KEY IDEAS IN TAX LAW

This book provides a short and clear guide to key ideas which underpin the UK tax code and illustrates the wider political and economic issues students need to know about when studying tax law. Some of these key ideas are controversial and the subject of much discussion and debate.

The book explains the key issues that are of fundamental juristic and philosophical importance and are common to tax codes throughout the world:

- What is a 'tax'?
- Is it different to a civil or criminal penalty?
- Why does this matter?
- Is 'taxation' necessarily a public law concept?
- Does the concept of 'taxation' attract constitutional considerations? Why? How do the answers to these questions play out when courts have to interpret tax provisions?

Readers will come away with a clear understanding of the architecture of the UK tax code, despite its (very real) complexity.

Key Ideas in Law: Volume 6

T0346993

Key Ideas in Law

Series Editor: Nicholas J McBride

Hart Publishing's series *Key Ideas in Law* offers short, stimulating introductions to legal subjects, providing an opportunity to step back from the detail of the law to consider its broader intellectual foundations and ideas, and how these work in practice.

Written by leading legal scholars with great expertise and depth of knowledge, these books offer an unparalleled combination of accessibility, concision, intellectual breadth and originality in legal writing.

Each volume will appeal to students seeking a concise introduction to a subject, stimulating wider reading for a course or deeper understanding for an exam, as well as to scholars and practitioners for the fresh perspectives and new ideas they provide.

Recent titles in this series:

Key Ideas in Contract Law
Nicholas J McBride

Key Ideas in Tort Law
Peter Cane

Key Ideas in Law: The Rule of Law and the Separation of Powers
Jack Beatson

Key Ideas in Trusts Law
Nicholas J McBride

Key Ideas in Commercial Law
William Day

Key Ideas in Tax Law
Julian Ghosh KC

For the complete list of titles in this series, see www.bloomsbury.com/uk/series/key-ideas-in-law/

Key Ideas in
Tax Law

Julian Ghosh KC

·H A R T·
OXFORD · LONDON · NEW YORK · NEW DELHI · SYDNEY

HART PUBLISHING

Bloomsbury Publishing Plc

Kemp House, Chawley Park, Cumnor Hill, Oxford, OX2 9PH, UK

1385 Broadway, New York, NY 10018, USA

29 Earlsfort Terrace, Dublin 2, Ireland

HART PUBLISHING, the Hart/Stag logo, BLOOMSBURY and the Diana logo are
trademarks of Bloomsbury Publishing Plc

First published in Great Britain 2024

Copyright © Julian Ghosh KC, 2024

A catalogue record for this book is available from the British Library.

A catalogue record for this book is available from the Library of Congress.

Library of Congress Control Number: 2024931646

ISBN: PB: 978-1-50995-073-7
       ePDF: 978-1-50995-075-1
       ePub: 978-1-50995-074-4

Typeset by Compuscript Ltd, Shannon
Printed and bound in Great Britain by CPI Group (UK) Ltd, Croydon CR0 4YY

To find out more about our authors and books visit www.hartpublishing.co.uk.
Here you will find extracts, author information, details of forthcoming events
and the option to sign up for our newsletters.

FOREWORD

LADY ROSE, JUSTICE OF THE UK SUPREME COURT

One of my responsibilities as President of the Upper Tribunal, Tax and Chancery Chamber was to sit on Judicial Appointments Commission selection panels to choose new tax judges. I recall an early briefing meeting with the non-legal panel members at which I was asked what kind of qualities we should be looking for in the candidates. I said that we were looking for someone who really *loves* tax law; who finds it continually fascinating and engaging; who enjoys wrestling with the most complicated statutory provisions and who has demonstrated that love and fascination by pursuing a legal career largely devoted to reading, debating and analysing tax law. My fellow panel members' eyebrows shot up with scepticism as to whether such people might exist. I assured them that we would know it when we saw it – and so it proved.

The reader of this small but important book, *Key Ideas in Tax Law*, would certainly recognise Dr Ghosh as someone with those qualities. His expert analytical skills combined with a long career at the pinnacle of the Tax Bar make him very well qualified to address the fundamental questions raised in the different chapters. The same can be said of the impressive cast of commentators who illuminate and advance the thesis of each chapter in their Responses.

Much of my work as a tax judge involves exploring the penumbra of everyday words. What exactly is a 'tunnel' for the purposes of the Capital Allowances Act 2001? What is a 'newspaper' for the purposes of the Value Added Tax Act 1994? What does it mean to 'discard' something for the purposes of the landfill tax charge? In this book, Dr Ghosh takes the tools of the tax lawyer's craft and deploys them to ask: what actually is 'tax' and what is tax for – or what should it be for? These questions prompt an examination of ideas drawn from the whole range of direct and indirect taxes. He illustrates his propositions with judicial authorities over the centuries and from different jurisdictions as well as drawing on the ideas of political philosophers past and present. The book raises in an erudite yet accessible way questions of the greatest importance to legislators, judges, practitioners, academics and students. There is useful material in the discussion of ideas with which we might think we are fully familiar. For example, although we all know that there must be a boundary between tax and other forms of monetary obligations, the discussion in chapter four of what makes tax distinct puts what might otherwise be dismissed as a gut feeling onto a firmer juridical basis. It teaches us some things we did not know about tax and may not have known about the other obligations discussed. That troublesome boundary between tax avoidance and tax mitigation is also put in a refreshing historical context, making it clear that judicial antipathy to tax avoidance did not start with *Ramsay* in 1981.

Taxes evoke strong feelings. From Charles I's attempts to raise ship money in 1634, to the Boston Tea Party in 1773 and to the Poll Tax protests in the 1990s, there is no doubt that everyone feels that they have some skin in the game when it comes to tax. This book invites us to lift our heads from the nitty gritty of particular taxes and look at the big picture. Everyone will find expert intellectual food for thought to interest and inform them in this book.

CONTENTS

ABBREVIATIONS OF STATUTES

CTA 2009	Corporation Tax Act 2009
CTA 2010	Corporation Tax Act 2010
IHTA 1984	Inheritance Tax Act 1984
ITA 2007	Income Tax Act 2007
ITEPA 2003	Income Tax (Earnings and Pensions) Act 2003
ITTOIA 2005	Income Tax (Trading and other Income) Act 2005
TCGA 1992	Taxation of Chargeable Gains Act 1992
TMA 1970	Taxes Management Act 1970
VATA 1994	Value Added Tax Act 1994

Introduction

Tax law is not always interesting. Tax law and books on tax law use words like 'computation'. But tax law can be interesting. Tax law punches above its weight in its contribution to the development of the law generally (its weight is considerable: the United Kingdom's tax legislation ('the UK tax code') is one of the longest in the world). Tax cases feature in administrative law (for example in relation to legitimate expectation (*R (MFK Underwriting Agents Ltd) v IRC* [1990] 1 WLR 1545); in trust law (*Vandervell v IRC* [1967] 2 AC 291) and in European Union (EU) law (*Cadbury Schweppes plc v IRC* [2007] Ch 30). And there are fundamental questions (which demand an answer) about tax law itself. 'What is a "tax"?' has become a sharp-edged legal question. Answering that question is a task worth undertaking both for the jurist and for the practitioner: see chapter four for answers to big constitutional issues which depend on this exercise being done.

This work is aimed at undergraduates who are studying law and are thinking of studying tax law, as an introduction, to demonstrate interesting issues of principle which tax law raises. It is also aimed at jurists, to demonstrate that tax law contributes answers to important questions which span many areas of law.

It seeks to put tax law (using illustrations from the UK tax code, although much of the analysis is jurisdictionally neutral) on a firm analytical base. It seeks to show that tax law is modal (that tax law has many different, perhaps conflicting, objectives, not a single function) but is nevertheless a distinct, coherent area of law, with recognisable juristic attributes. Tax law, like many juristic concepts (such as 'property'), does have a central or core meaning. That meaning may be modified in a particular statutory context but this does not mean that tax has no core meaning at all. This work identifies the central features of a 'tax', which may then be subjected to statutory modification in a specific area.

This book identifies the basic building blocks of tax law and the important (key) ideas embedded *within* it (chapter one). Thereafter, the work discusses key ideas *about* tax law, which apply in a very particular way to tax (chapters three to five). Much of the philosophical work considering taxation does not appreciate the juristic nature of a tax obligation, which this work also discusses (chapter six). Readers will find their understanding enhanced and provoked by the short responses to each chapter by senior academics and professionals, including judges (some exceptionally occupy more than one category with great distinction).

The key ideas within tax law and about tax law discussed in this book will, it is hoped, provoke interest, debate and further work. There are three important points to note.

First, tax obligations in the UK are all personal monetary obligations. Many of the observations of principle made in this book flow from this. To the extent that a tax is ever legislated as a proprietary debt, many of the observations might be different, or fall away.

Second, taxes are different to other extractions of property and monies from those within the jurisdiction of the extractor, even where these latter extractions might have identical objectives to tax (this follows from the modal nature of tax, set out in chapter two). Because an area of law has the same objective as tax does not make it part of tax law. I disagree with those who say that the notion of 'tax' includes some or all extractive mechanisms which have the effect of requiring a person to make over property or monies. Readers will have to take a view as to which approach they find more persuasive (this is the point of this book).

Third, I have taken illustrations of taxes from the UK tax code (income tax on trades, capital gains tax, inheritance tax and Value Added Tax), all of which are uncontroversially 'taxes'. The big message is that the model of a 'tax' charge in chapter one holds good for all 'taxes', including customs duties and the like (this is a challenge to the reader). So it may be that readers will agree with my conclusions for 'uncontroversial taxes' which impose personal monetary obligations but reserve judgement on whether there may be more to say and disagree with, with other obligations they consider to be 'taxes' but I do not. So be it. The more that this book promotes agreement or disagreement in contexts that matter (academic study, decisions made in courts) the more successful it will have been in achieving its aim. Tax law is, in fact, a repository of big legal ideas. It is hoped that scholars and jurists find something in this book to inspire more thinking and find satisfaction and interest in tax law.

1

What is Tax?

1. THE STRUCTURE OF A TAX CHARGE: A MODEL

What is a 'tax', legally speaking? This chapter sets out a model of a tax charge, that is, its component parts. These are the notions of a 'taxable' person, 'tax' base, 'taxable' amount, 'tax' rate and 'tax' compliance and enforcement. There is a theoretical prospect of common law taxes (that is, taxes with a non-statutory source), although there is no actual example of a common law tax in the UK tax code. To accommodate this theoretical prospect, the model discusses the analytical components of a 'tax' charge without any reference to the nature of the body which imposes or collects the tax. There is no need to define tax by reference to any 'public' body which legislates for or enforces tax laws. However, given that there is no actual example of a common law tax in the UK tax code, any reference to 'rules' is a reference to statutory rules. And to repeat an observation in the introduction, tax law, like many juristic concepts (such as 'property'), has a core meaning. That meaning may be modified in a particular statutory context but this does not mean that tax has no core meaning at all. So the model of a 'tax' discussed below is not an exercise in sterile essentialism but an exercise of discovery, to identify what that core meaning is.

Let us say that 'swimming' is defined as propelling oneself through the water using arms and legs (somehow). It follows that any venue in which swimming takes place may be properly called 'swimming' baths, an instructor a 'swimming' instructor, and so on. What emerges from the model below is that, for every 'tax', there is a person subject to that charge (a 'taxable person') and a something that the taxable person does (a 'taxable activity'). These terms may be identified in a way which applies for all taxes. One or both of a taxable person and a taxable activity will have attributes which may ('may', not 'does' as a taxable activity may result in a loss) produce (in combination) an amount, a 'taxable amount', which in turn yields an obligation to pay monies, a 'tax charge'.

The model set out in this chapter establishes the attributes needed for a person to be a 'taxable' person, for that something done to be a 'taxable activity' and for an amount of money to be a 'taxable' amount, on which a computation results in an obligation on a taxable person to pay monies: if all these components can be identified, we have a 'tax' charge.

Incidentally and importantly, this work uses the term 'taxable activity' as a term which encompasses anything done by a taxable person (whether active, such as trading, or passive, such as holding an investment, or indeed, the mere receipt of income such as an annuity) which is relevant in computing a 'taxable amount'. The term 'activity' is not restricted to somehow 'earning' a reward, as opposed to receiving passive investment income. It extends to anything done which generates a 'taxable amount'. This is important, as some tax codes, including the UK tax code, historically taxed 'earned income' (from active sources, such as trades) less harshly than 'unearned income' (passive investment income, such as dividends, or interest). The term 'activity' in this work covers both the generation of earned income and unearned income, in other words, anything done which generates a 'taxable amount' for any tax.

All of a taxable person, a taxable activity (in its wide sense) and a 'taxable amount' are necessary components of a tax charge, for any tax. A taxable activity is not an intelligible legal concept without a taxable person who is subject to a charge on that taxable activity. And a tax charge pre-supposes that there may be an amount, which must have some rational connection to both the taxable person and the taxable activity, which is a 'taxable amount' on which the ultimate tax charge is computed. The legal identification of each of these component parts results in a complete, distinct set of legal rules which comprises a 'tax charge'. Any compliance and enforcement mechanisms which apply to the money obligation to pay a taxable amount are part of separate legal rules which police and enforce 'tax' obligations and to 'tax' debts. And a body which imposes or enforces such an obligation is a 'taxing' body. Thus, to adapt the language of public international lawyers, certainly in the case of a tax charge imposed by statute, the imposition of a tax charge is an exercise of legislative prescriptive jurisdiction (which is supplemented by a separate enforcement jurisdiction of the body entitled to secure satisfaction, by the imposition of compliance and enforcement obligations). And as made clear in chapter four, a tax obligation arising from an exercise of prescriptive jurisdiction is distinct from other impositions, such as penalties, fines and tortious damages.

This model assumes that 'tax' is, one way or another, an imposition. Any tax obligation arises by an exercise of prescriptive jurisdiction (laying aside for the moment the prospect of common law taxes). Tax is not a voluntary payment, or the result of a bargain where two or more parties seek to progress their commercial interests in a mutually agreed way. A work on tax law necessarily deals with legal norms. 'Tax law' comprises those legal norms which impose a money obligation on a particular person (a 'taxable person'). This is intuitively correct; see the, albeit imperfect but not on this point, Oxford English Dictionary definition of a tax as 'a compulsory contribution to the support of government …' famously referred to in *Tiley's Revenue Law* now in its 10th edition by Glen Loutzenhiser (Loutzenhiser 2022). It is also consistent with the examples of actual taxes in the UK tax code discussed below.

2. A TAXABLE PERSON

Every 'tax' charge fixes an obligation to pay monies ('tax') on a particular person. Otherwise, the very notion of a 'tax charge' makes no sense. A taxable person is identified by (1) that person carrying on a particular activity (a 'putative taxable activity', in that the activity is, in law, capable of giving rise to a tax charge but will only actually be 'taxable' if the person satisfies the next condition: 'activity' is used in its wide sense) *and* (2) that person having some connecting factor(s) to the jurisdiction of the authority which seeks to impose a charge on that person. Such connecting factors may be an attribute of the person or the way or nature in which an activity is undertaken in the jurisdiction. Both are necessary conditions, 'trigger' conditions, which must be satisfied for a person to be a 'taxable person'. Neither the carrying on of the putative taxable activity, nor possession of the connecting factors alone will make a person a 'taxable person'. Both trigger conditions must be met.

This terminology of 'putative taxable activity' is the writer's. It is a useful term as it makes clear that an activity contemplated by any tax code to be a 'taxable activity' only becomes a 'taxable activity' in law if it results in a charge on some 'taxable person'; one must look to see if that person is indeed a 'taxable person' before identifying an activity as a 'taxable activity': hence the activity is only a 'putative taxable activity' until a 'taxable person' has been identified.

The identification of 'putative taxable activities' is relatively straight-forward. These will be specified in any particular tax code which purports to impose a 'tax' (if a particular activity is not so specified, it cannot be a putative taxable activity; if it is so specified, it will be a putative taxable activity, so long as it is capable of producing a taxable amount in the hands of a taxable person). Also, a putative taxable activity must, in some way, result in the computation of an amount which is a 'taxable amount' in the hands of a taxable person. If the rules which specify a particular activity as giving rise to a 'tax' charge do not provide for that activity to give rise to a taxable amount (for example, if that activity is exempted from any charge), that activity cannot be a putative taxable activity. To identify a putative taxable activity is easy where a person tries to make money: examples of such putative taxable activities are the carrying on of a trade, the receipt of investment income and the realisation of invest-ment assets. But even where a particular tax taxes amounts given away, such as inheritance tax (IHT), the taxable amount for the taxable person is that gifted amount (which IHT disincentivises: of course, that gift is very much a reward for the donee-recipient but IHT considers that for its purposes the relevant taxable amount is computed in the hands of the donor, being the amount of the gift).

Generally, the taxable person will be the person who undertakes the putative taxable activity, although there are exceptional counter-examples: so an interest in possession beneficiary of a trust where the trustees undertake the putative taxable activity is the taxable person for income tax purposes on any income arising from that activity; there are very few, if any, other examples where the person who undertakes the taxable activity, whether alone or with others, is not the taxable person.

What of the necessary connecting factors? Connecting factors try to legitimise the exercise of 'taxing' jurisdiction over a person (making them a 'taxable person'). While, in the UK, absolute continuing Parliamentary sovereignty theoretically entitles the UK to tax an Australian trader who sells widgets as part of a purely Australian trade to an Australian purchaser, where neither seller nor buyer has any connection to the UK, this is neither practically sensible, nor, according to some, legally permissible in international law (see Vann 1996). In public international law, the overwhelming consensus is that a 'reasonable connection' (applying the principle of 'territoriality') must exist between a taxing authority and any person whom it wishes to tax: see Mann 1964, Vol. 1, 109–19; Mann 1984 Vol. 2, 28–30; Albrecht 1952; and Martha 1989, 12–18. So *some* connecting factor is generally required to make the seller of these widgets a 'taxable person' (even though the sale of widgets is a putative 'taxable activity').

A jurisdiction has a choice of selecting whatever connecting factors it wishes. In theory (and in practice for some jurisdictions, such as the United States), citizenship might be one: a jurisdiction may legislate to provide that any citizen, wherever located in the world, must pay 'tax' on specified (putative taxable) activities. There are examples of the UK taxing those with only a short and fleeting connection to the UK (for example, see, in relation to income tax on foreign entertainers and sportsmen, the Income Tax (Trading and other Income) Act 2005 ('ITTOIA 2005'), section 13 and *Agassi v Robinson* [2006] STC 1056). However, the UK has generally recognised territoriality as a legal presumption which accepts the practical limitations of enforcement as informing the scope of taxing legislation (*Ex parte Blain* (1879) 12 Ch D 522; *Clark v Oceanic Contractors Inc* [1983] STC 35, at 43 (per Lord Scarman): '[the issue is whether a person has] made himself subject to United Kingdom [in this case tax] jurisdiction …'). The UK does not use citizenship as a connecting factor but (like many other jurisdictions) applies territoriality through, for income tax and capital gains tax purposes, the notions of 'tax residence' and 'source'. Other (different) connecting factors apply for other taxes, such as IHT and Value Added Tax (VAT). In all cases, the connecting factors are either attributes of a taxable person or the nature of the putative taxable activity. It is worth examining tax residence and source which apply for income tax purposes to see territoriality in action, although, the requirement of *some* connecting factor (not necessarily residence or source) between a person and the relevant jurisdiction for that person to be a 'taxable person' applies in principle for all taxes (as it is a function of public international law) and in fact applies to all of the actual taxes in the UK tax code discussed below.

In relation to tax 'residence', the taxing rights of a particular state for income tax are legitimised because of a personal or legal connection between that State and a particular person. In the case of individuals, the notion of 'residence' may be defined by reference to facts and circumstances which attach to that individual, such as physical presence in the taxing state, economic ties and habitual abode. Of course, there are other possible connecting factors for income tax and other taxes (there is no exhaustive list). For income tax, in relation to legal entities (non-natural persons), residence may be defined, for example, by reference to the place of incorporation, statutory seat, the place of central management and control and/or place of effective management.

A different connecting factor, 'source', establishes the legitimacy of the imposition of income tax not because of the characteristics attaching to a particular person but rather because the activity has a sufficiently strong and relevant connection to the source state (for example, trading in a jurisdiction through a fixed place of business or via an agent). What is 'relevant' and of sufficient strength may vary from tax to tax: different notions of source may apply, for example, to income tax on trading and import duties. But once established, this is enough to make the person undertaking that putative taxable activity a 'taxable person' (albeit that that person may not have any other connection to the taxing state) and the taxable amount arising from that activity (however defined) subject to tax in the source state. Importantly, it is not the carrying out of a particular activity in itself which makes that activity 'taxable' but carrying it out 'in' (in a sufficiently strong and relevant sense) a particular location which attracts an obligation to pay. This 'location' condition is conceptually additional to the carrying on of the activity (and is a connecting factor distinct from the putative taxable activity). The notion of 'source' could, in theory, be extended to capture any putative taxable activity which has even a weak connection to the source state but the orthodox notion of source roots the legitimacy of taxing a putative taxable activity, in the hands of a non-source state resident person, in there being a strong and relevant connection between the actual activity on the one hand and the source state on the other.

So, for instance, for income tax purposes, it is not enough that a non-UK resident (non-corporate) person undertakes a trade (a putative taxable activity); that non-UK resident trader is only a 'taxable person' insofar as the trade is carried on 'in' the UK: Income Tax (Trading and Other Income) Act 2005, section 6. The same is broadly true for a trading non-UK resident company, which is a 'taxable person' only insofar as trading profits are attributable to a 'permanent establishment' (being broadly a fixed place of business or agency) in the UK: Corporation Tax Act 2009, section 5, Corporation Tax Act 2010, section 1141. And for interest received as investment income by a non-UK resident, the non-UK resident is only a 'taxable person' to the extent that the interest has a UK 'source', held to be the function of a 'multi-factorial' test, which includes the residence of the debtor and place of enforcement: *Westminster Bank Executor and Trustee v National Bank of Greece* [1971] AC 945.

The relevant connecting factors, as a matter of principle, not only establish the right of a jurisdiction to impose a charge on a person but may also have the effect of increasing the scope of the putative taxable activities which become taxable activities. In relation to income tax, for example, orthodoxy dictates that a tax resident person is taxable on all their worldwide income and investment profits ('unlimited taxation'), while non-residents are taxable only on profits arising from sources located within that state ('limited taxation'). For a 'tax resident' taxable person, their worldwide putative taxable activities become 'taxable activities', whereas for a person who is a taxable person only because they have a source of profits located within the jurisdiction of the charge-imposing body, their only taxable activity is the activity which yields those profits. The importance of these relevant connecting factors in principle becomes highly visible. Lord Wrenbury explained this in *Whitney v IRC* [1926] AC 37, at 54 by reference to a perceived quid pro quo for benefits received:

> The policy of the [United Kingdom Income Tax Acts] is to tax the person resident in the United Kingdom upon all his income whencesoever derived, and to tax the person not resident in the United Kingdom upon all income derived from property in the United Kingdom. The former is taxed because (whether he be a British subject or not) he enjoys the benefit of our laws with the protection of his person and his property. The latter is taxed because in respect of his property in the United Kingdom he enjoys the benefit of our laws for the protection of that property.

This rationale for the distinction between unlimited and limited taxation for income tax is questionable. For natural persons and their property, citizenship, rather than tax residence, is more likely to confer the protection of a particular state (and generate allegiance) at least outside the territory of the state. For legal persons, in particular companies, tax residence is generally defined by reference to (alternatively) the place of incorporation (Corporation Tax Act 2009, section 14(1)) and the location of central management and control (*De Beers v Consolidated Mines Ltd v Howe* [1906] AC 455), making the link between a liability to tax and protection by or allegiance to a particular taxing state even more tenuous. Furthermore, this explanation of the conventional connecting factors betrays a type of 'benefits' analysis (see Cooper 1994 for a summary of 'benefits theory' analysis), which has long since been discredited, for example by John Stuart Mill as offensive to distributive justice (see Mill 1909, Book V, Chapter 2, paragraph [2]):

> If there were any justice, therefore, in the [benefits] theory of justice now under consideration, those who are least capable of helping or defending themselves, being those to whom the protection of government is the most indispensable, ought to pay the greatest share of its price: the reverse of the true idea of distributive justice, which consists not in imitating but in re-dressing the inequalities and wrongs of nature.

Nevertheless, the notions of residence and source as necessary connecting factors to identify a taxable person for income tax purposes are firmly embedded in the UK tax code (see *Colquhoun v Brooks* (1883–1890) 2 TC 490, 499 (per Lord Herschell), approved in *National Bank of Greece SA v Westminster Bank Executor and Trustee Co (Channel Islands) Ltd* [1971] AC 945, 954). The principle was endorsed by the House of Lords in *Clark v Oceanic Contractors Inc* [1983] STC 35, at 45–46 (per Lord Wilberforce). Territoriality fundamentally informs the construction of the UK tax code: ibid, 43 (per Lord Scarman).

As explained above, other taxes in the UK tax code adopt different connecting factors. Examples include IHT and VAT, which are examined below. What is important is the claim made in this chapter that every tax must (to produce a 'tax charge') identify a taxable person, a putative taxable activity and a taxable amount. A challenge to the reader is to identify a 'tax' which does not fit this model.

Some final thoughts on connecting factors (for all taxes, including those for income tax discussed here) are worth airing: particular connecting factors may be found to conflict with other, hierarchically superior laws. So, during the UK's membership of the EU, 'residence' and 'source' as connecting factors for income tax, which not only defined a 'taxable person' but also informed access to tax reliefs, were held to be (at times, subject to proportionate justification) contrary to the internal market provisions of the Treaty of the Functioning of the European Union. Further, in the technologically sophisticated world of the twenty-first century, it is increasingly questionable whether these particular connecting factors are sufficiently flexible to fix taxing jurisdiction on persons who are neither tax resident within a particular jurisdiction, nor have a source of taxable receipts within that jurisdiction, using commercial methods which may not give rise to a taxable 'source' (for example because the commercial methods employed do not amount to a 'permanent establishment'). These are questions for another day. But these important questions arise because of the fundamental importance of identifying some connecting factor between a person and a taxing jurisdiction, whether through the attributes of the person themselves or the strength of the connection.

We may now turn to the other 'key ideas' within tax: the 'tax' base (which yields a 'taxable' amount), 'tax' rates and 'tax' compliance and enforcement provisions.

3. THE TAX BASE (COMPUTATION OF A 'TAXABLE AMOUNT')

The section above identifies whether there is a taxable person (with connecting factors and a putative taxable activity). We may now go on to identify whether there is a 'taxable amount'. In the hands of a taxable person, the putative taxable activity becomes a taxable activity, which can yield a taxable amount.

In principle, given that each of a taxable person, a taxable activity and a taxable amount must be identified to give rise to a 'tax charge', conceptually, one could start any interrogation of whether there is a tax charge by asking first whether a (putative) taxable activity yields a 'taxable amount' and then identify whether there is a 'taxable person'. After all, the fixing of an obligation to pay this charge ('assessment to tax') could be (theoretically) on anyone (depending on how the connecting factors are defined).

This order of analysis would make visible the different sub-rules which apply to the computation of a taxable amount and the identification of (an assessment to tax of) a taxable person. But the identification of a taxable person and of the putative taxable activity go hand in hand. They must be both identified for a tax charge to arise, along with a taxable amount computed on the putative taxable activity (if no taxable amount arises because of, say an exemption, there is obviously no 'tax' charge). It is more analytically convenient to identify whether there is a taxable person and then identify whether a taxable activity yields a taxable amount.

Put another way, because the identification of a taxable person, a taxable activity (and the tax base) and a taxable amount are all necessary components of a tax charge, if no person is identified as the person who is obliged to pay a charge, there is, quite simply, no relevant 'taxable' activity.

This is why it is once (and only once) a taxable person is identified, a 'tax' charge can arise in respect of a taxable amount computed on that taxable person's 'tax base'. Not because a tax code must adopt this chronology of analysis (the UK tax code does not) but rather because, as observed above, it is in the hands of a taxable person, that the putative taxable activity is now a 'taxable' activity.

The tax base of any tax is the result of (1) identifying those taxable activities undertaken by a taxable person (for example, whether the person is undertaking a 'trade', where a trade is the taxable activity), (2) identifying which amounts (subject to any permitted deductions) are relevant to computing the taxable person's tax charge on those taxable activities (for example, where the taxable activity is 'trading', which amounts are taxable 'trading receipts') and then (3) specifying how positive amounts and any deductions from those positive amounts are measured. A specified period of time (depending on the particular tax) will determine which taxable receipts and permitted deductions are relevant for a particular computation. The measurement mechanism for the taxable amount may, for instance, follow accounting treatment, perhaps qualified and supplemented in statute, or a cash basis which simply tracks the receipt and expenditure of cash sums.

That tax base computation will determine a net positive amount (a 'taxable amount'), by way of the combined effect of 'charging provisions' and 'relieving' or exemption provisions. If permitted deductions exceeds taxable receipts, the deficit may or may not be set against other taxable receipts, depending on the tax. The identification of a taxable activity thus has a dual role: a definitional role (as a putative taxable activity, to identify the taxable person) and (conceptually separately) a computational role (to provide a tax base to which rules of measurement and computation of taxable receipts and deductible amounts may be applied to yield a taxable amount).

The computation of relevant amounts (less allowed deductions), properly measured, will result in a 'taxable amount' for the taxable person. Importantly, this taxable amount must, to be described as 'taxable', have a relevant and rational connection to the taxable person. Their taxable activity and connecting factors which legitimise the imposition and enforcement of the obligation: see chapter four for amounts which are correctly described as 'penalties' which have a connection to the taxable activity but not to relevant connecting factors and are thus best described as amounts computed 'by reference to a taxable amount' rather than as actual 'taxable amounts'. If the relevant amount is not relevantly and rationally a function of a person who is a 'taxable' person and an activity which becomes a 'taxable' activity, it cannot be a 'taxable' amount.

Embedded within this key idea of the tax base is the central notion that 'tax' (any tax) is about monetary amounts; the money debt is non-proprietary (see further in chapter three), so that all the creditor (that is, the tax authority) can insist upon is the receipt of an amount of money, not the receipt of *particular* monies, say a portion of the taxable person's trading receipts, or turnover. In other words, a tax charge does not fix upon any particular assets of a taxable person. This insight has crucial implications for the juristic character of tax (see chapter three) and how tax is to be theorised philosophically (see chapter six). It is this non-proprietary nature of tax which distinguishes tax from compulsory acquisitions of property. If tax were levied on a proprietary basis, to be sure, the analysis of the conceptual implication of a tax charge would change, perhaps a lot. But generally it is not, either in the UK tax code or in other jurisdictions. (To take three examples, in the United States, 26 USC 6151 establishes that the taxes it covers are personal, non-proprietary monetary obligations; the same is true of Germany (German Fiscal Code, section 48(1)); and South Africa (Tax Administration Act 2011, section 162).)

4. THE SETTING OF A TAX RATE

Having established who is the taxable person and identified the tax base and any taxable amount, the 'tax charge' on a taxable person, in respect of a particular taxable activity, is the amount which arises after the relevant 'tax rate' is applied to the taxable amount. This provides the tax payable by the taxable person.

A tax rate may be 'flat' (so all taxable persons have the same rate applied to their taxable amounts), 'proportionate' or 'progressive'. A flat tax rate is 'regressive', since it necessarily has a greater impact on the less wealthy, while proportionate and progressive rates assume that the wealthier a taxable person is, the more they can properly be asked to pay in tax. A proportional tax ensures the same percentage of tax is taken from all, irrespective of wealth (so that the wealthier pay more tax in absolute terms precisely because their wealth is greater); a progressive tax increases the *percentage* of tax charged as a taxpayer falls into higher wealth categories (so that the wealthier pay more in both absolute and proportional terms). The rate of tax applied to each additional pound of income is that taxable person's 'marginal rate'. The body which imposes and enforces payment of this tax may thus be properly called a 'taxing' body or authority.

5. TAX COMPLIANCE AND TAX ENFORCEMENT

The identification of a taxable person, a tax base and a taxable amount all arise from an exercise of a prescriptive jurisdiction. The charge to tax is a complete legal obligation once these components have been identified.

Separately, although of course connected, a tax code unsurprisingly generally imposes obligations on certain persons (those identified as being, or who may be, taxable persons and perhaps others, such as agents) to make appropriate returns to the taxing authority, to police the tax code, making sure that the taxing authority has visibility on those persons (and to identify which of those persons are taxable persons undertaking taxable activities which produce taxable amounts). These obligations are 'tax compliance obligations'. Once a tax rate has been applied to a taxable amount (for a particular taxable activity), the 'tax charge' payable crystalises into a monetary debt owed to the taxing authority. This is one complete set of laws, arising from an exercise of prescriptive jurisdiction. The enforcement of tax is the enforcement of a money debt, a distinct exercise of enforcement jurisdiction, if a taxable person does not pay their tax debt in time.

Such compliance and enforcement obligations have an internal relationship to the provisions which define a taxable person, a taxable activity and a taxable amount (in that compliance and enforcement provisions make sense only in relation to those provisions which give rise to a debt in the first place). But this internal relationship is very different to the relationship that the provisions which define a taxable person, a taxable activity and a taxable amount have with each other. These latter provisions are analogous to defining the actions which a person's limbs make in propelling them through water to swim, in defining 'swimming'. Compliance and enforcement provisions are analogous to the fee that person must pay to enter the venue and the rules of behaviour they must observe when they enter. These latter provisions, being an exercise of enforcement jurisdiction, represent what a taxable person must do once prescriptive jurisdiction has established that a person is indeed a taxable person who has a tax charge on a taxable amount.

Furthermore, as discussed here and in chapter three, for UK taxes (at least those discussed here and in fact all taxes imposed in the UK) this money debt is a non-proprietary debt due to the Crown. Such a 'tax' charge is thus an obligation on a taxpayer to deliver money to satisfy the debt, no more, no less. That the tax charge is a personal money obligation proves extremely important to the key ideas discussed in the following chapters.

There is nothing in the analytical definitions of 'taxable person', 'taxable activity', or 'taxable amount' which necessitates that the tax charge be a personal, non-proprietary debt. It is theoretically possible for a tax charge to be legislated as a proprietary debt, fixing proprietorial rights on a taxable person's property in the exercise of either prescriptive jurisdiction or enforcement jurisdiction. This type of tax charge would be exigible on a taxable person's particular property (say particular monies received from the counterparty to a taxable activity). Some of the analytical conclusions made below would be very different for such a tax charge. However, there is no example of such a tax charge in the UK and although this point should be borne in mind, it is flagged, rather than addressed in any depth, in the relevant chapters below.

6. A SUMMARY OF THE MODEL'S CONCLUSIONS

THE MODEL IS COMPREHENSIVE

All tax provisions in the UK tax code, even the most complicated, may be identified and explained as doing one of the following things: defining a taxable person, defining a tax base (which yields a taxable amount) and defining tax compliance/enforcement obligations. To anticipate a discussion on 'tax avoidance' below and in chapter five, take an 'anti-avoidance' provision. The UK tax code considers that if a settlor settles property on trust (or indeed effects any 'arrangements' relating to the property) but is able (in any way at all) to benefit from that settled property, any tax charge on income or investment gains on a taxable activity from that property should fall on the settlor, not on the trustees: ITTOIA 2005, sections 624, 625. The UK tax code considers that the potential benefit to the settlor means that the settlor is taxed on their marginal rates, rather than the trustees at their (lower) marginal rates. These provisions can be readily integrated into the model provided above: they identify the settlor as a 'taxable person' and treat a settlement of property where the trustees undertake a putative taxable activity but in which settlor retains a (potential) benefit as a special type of taxable activity (avoidance) attributed to the settlor. The challenge to the reader is to, on the one hand, identify a 'tax' which they say does not fit the model, or, on the other hand, identify something which they consider to be a 'tax' which does not fit the model and explain why this obligation is indeed a 'tax'.

'TAX LAW': COHERENT AND DISTINCT

The model set out above presents tax law as a readily identifiable area of law, distinct from other areas of law which impose money debts. The juristic attributes (and the rules of a tax code which give them legal form) of a 'taxable' person, the identification of a 'tax' base, the computation of a 'tax' charge, the satisfaction of 'tax' compliance obligations and the imposition of a money debt by a 'taxing' authority may be described, adapting the terminology of Professor Joseph Raz, as an 'internal' relationship: Raz 1980, 24. These rules depend on each other for relevance: they make no sense in isolation. And they form the component parts of a single, distinct set of rules which define a 'tax charge' (which set of rules would be incomplete if one or more of these components were missing).

These notions are specific to tax law, in that the definition of a 'taxable' person by reference to a putative taxable activity and to relevant connecting factors apply to a specific charge imposed by specific rules. Of course, these connecting factors may and do vary from tax to tax. But a tax charge will be the function of the exercise of prescriptive jurisdiction which identifies each of a taxable person, a tax base and a taxable amount (to which a tax rate will apply). This is what distinguishes 'tax' from other money debts imposed under different rules (say a charge to visit museums, which arises under contract between the museum goer and the museum, not a prescriptive jurisdiction), or a parking fine (which penalises and enforces a distinct, different, prohibitory rule: see chapter four). This is what tells us that tax law is both coherent (comprising intelligible concepts) and distinct from other areas of law, at least at the level of principle.

It is also important to note at this stage that these attributes hold good (and tax law as an area of law remains distinct and coherent) with no reference at all to any particular objective of particular taxes (which are many and diverse: see below). But tax law is still a coherent and distinct area of law. This flows from the model set out above. This key idea is developed further in chapter four. Chapter two explains the modal nature of taxation; that is, that taxation has diverse objectives. This model applies whatever the objective of a particular tax may be.

7. FURTHER PARASITIC KEY IDEAS WITHIN TAX LAW

There are further ideas, which, one way or another, refine the fundamental key ideas of 'taxable person', 'tax base', 'taxable amount', 'tax rate' and 'tax' compliance and enforcement obligations within tax law. These are 'parasitic' ideas of tax law: none of them would make sense except by reference to these fundamental key ideas, and a 'tax' charge may be imposed without any appeal to one or more of them. Nevertheless, these further ideas are important enough to be themselves 'key ideas' within tax law.

'DIRECT' VERSUS 'INDIRECT' TAXES

The monetary nature of a tax obligation permits a distinction between 'direct' or 'indirect' taxes. John Stuart Mill distinguishes 'direct' and 'indirect' taxes as follows (Mill 1909, Book V, Chapter 3):

> A direct tax is one which is demanded from the very persons who it is intended or desired should pay it. Indirect taxes are those which are demanded from one person in the *expectation and intention* that he shall indemnify himself at the expense of the other: such as the excise or the customs. The producer or importer of a commodity is called upon to pay a tax on it, not with the intention to levy a peculiar contribution upon him, but to tax through him the consumers of the commodity, from whom it is supposed that he will recover the amount by means of an advance in price. (emphasis added)

Mill's distinction between direct and indirect taxes has judicial endorsement, where the vires for levying tax was restricted to 'indirect' taxes: *Bank of Toronto v Lambe* [1887] 12 AC 575, *Brewers & Maltsters of Ontario v Attorney-General for Ontario* [1897] AC 231, discussed in *Charles S Cotton v The King* [1914] AC 176 at 192, 193 (per Lord Moulton); *Re Eurig* [1998] 2 SCR 565, [25]–[26]. Examples of direct taxes are income tax, capital gains tax and corporation tax. There is a legislative assumption that the burden of the tax will be suffered by the person on whom the formal liability lies.

By contrast, VAT is a classic 'indirect' tax, where the legislative intention is the burden borne by the ultimate consumer: *Elida Gibbs v Customs and Excise Commissioners* [1997] QB 499. Say the seller of widgets is taxed to VAT (see below) at a rate of 20 per cent of the sale price, and is content with a sale price of £100. That seller can simply add £20 to that sale price, so that the purchaser pays £120. The seller receives £120, keeps the £100 they are happy with and pays the taxing authority £20 in VAT. The purchaser has borne the burden of the VAT of £20, although the formal obligation to pay is on the seller. This is the legislative assumption that underpins VAT: the system of permitted deductions from the amount to be paid in tax assumes that the final consumer will bear the burden of VAT in the purchase price and that all the participants in the chain of production and distribution will not suffer any burden at all. In the simple example given here, the seller has not suffered any loss at all by the VAT charge: they have simply passed this cost onto the purchaser. That is not to say that the burden of a 'direct' tax, such as income tax, cannot be shifted. For example, an employee may well negotiate net-of-tax wages. The dividing line between direct and indirect taxes is porous. The status of a tax as 'indirect' will be a function of the 'expectation and intention' of the legislator, as opposed to the parties to a transaction, which may not always be easy to determine.

'FORMAL' AND 'EFFECTIVE' 'INCIDENCE' OF TAX

The distinction between 'direct' and 'indirect' taxes can also be expressed as a distinction between the 'formal' and 'effective' incidence of a tax charge. The formal incidence of tax is a matter of who is legally liable to pay the tax or from whom the tax is collected, whereas the effective incidence of tax is concerned with who ultimately bears the burden of the tax. Indeed, the very distinction between direct and indirect taxes is only possible by reason of the prospect of the formal and effective incidence of a liability to tax being different, which in turn is a direct function of a liability to taxation being a money (and not a property) liability (see further in chapter three).

HYPOTHECATION OF TAXES

A tax is 'hypothecated' if the monies raised by that tax are expressly earmarked for a specific purpose. Of course, tax revenues may be used for a specific purpose (for example, to fund the National Health Service) and a government may advertise this, but there is no example of a tax within the UK tax code which must in law be used for a particular purpose.

'ALLOWANCES', 'RELIEFS' AND 'EXEMPTIONS' FROM TAX

These all affect the ultimate tax rate for a taxable person. An 'allowance' is an amount on which a taxable person need not pay tax: this amount is entered into the tax computation as an amount excluded from tax. Examples are the 'personal allowance' for income tax (Income Tax Act 2007 (ITA 2007), section 35), which assumes that all taxable persons must have a minimum amount for subsistence (this is now lost when a taxpayer's income reaches a certain level), a similar 'personal allowance' that applies in the context of capital gains tax (CGT) (Taxation of Chargeable Gains Act 1992 (TCGA 1992), section 1K), and the nil-rate band in the case of IHT (Inheritance Tax Act 1984 (IHTA 1984), Schedule 1).

There is a 'relief' from tax where the UK tax code reduces or eliminates an amount from a charge to tax. Examples of 'reliefs' include loss relief where one year's trading losses may be used against another year's trading profits (ITA 2007, section 83), relief from CGT where a taxable person disposes of an asset which is favoured by the UK tax code, for example shares (of at least a 10 per cent holding) in a trading company (TCGA 1992, Part V, Chapter 3), or relief from IHT where a 'transfer of value' for IHT purposes is reduced to the extent that the property is a trading asset (IHTA 1984, section 112).

An exemption excludes amounts from the tax computation altogether.

'WITHHOLDING TAXES'

The UK tax code (in common with other jurisdictions) often imposes withholding taxes. These are generally imposed for practical reasons. Take, for example, income tax on employment receipts: the employee is the taxable person, but the monies (say salary) are paid by the employer to (often) many employees. It is more efficient for the UK tax code to require the payer of those monies to withhold the tax due by all of the employee-payees (the employee-taxable persons) and pay this over to HMRC, rather than to scrutinise the tax computations of a large number of employees. This system (for employment income, 'Pay-As-You-Earn', or 'PAYE') is a 'withholding tax'. The 'taxable person' is the employee, but the payer (the employer) effectively behaves as a tax collector and must withhold and pay over the taxable amount to the taxing authority: Income Tax (Earnings and Pensions) Act 2003, Part 11. Withholding tax is also often imposed on cross border payments, on the basis that the non-tax resident recipient should bear tax on the payment, which is, for efficiency, withheld at the time of payment by the payer.

'DOUBLE TAXATION'

Receipts (actual or deemed) may be subject to tax more than once. Examples of 'double taxation' are actual ('economic') or 'juridical' in nature.

Say a trading company makes £100 as a trading profit (a 'taxable amount') and pays corporation tax on that £100 at 20 per cent, leaving £80, which the company pays as a dividend to Ms X, its shareholder. Ms X has a taxable amount of £80. Say Ms X has a tax rate of 45 per cent on the dividend (leaving her £44). Tax law generally treats the company's taxable amount of £100 as a different taxable amount in the hands of the company to Ms X's taxable amount on the dividend of £80. If Ms X pays 45 per cent income tax on the dividend, the £100 would be taxed twice, once at 20 per cent in the hands of the company and again (albeit only £80) at 45 per cent in Ms X's hands because the company pays the dividend out of 'taxed income'. This is economic double taxation. It is sometimes (not always) cured by a whole or partial credit or exemption for a recipient of monies paid out of taxed income.

Juridical double taxation is different. Say a taxable person who is tax resident in Germany receives UK source income (such as interest). Both Germany (the state of residence) and the UK (the source state) may tax this amount, while respecting territoriality. 'Double tax treaties' (usually bilateral between signatory state) generally (but not always) avoid juridical double taxation and ensure that only one state taxes the interest. Furthermore, the UK has its own rules, applicable in the absence of double tax treaties, that are designed to limit the possibility of double taxation in certain cases: Taxation (International and Other Provisions) Act 2010, Part 2, Chapter 1.

TAX MITIGATION, TAX AVOIDANCE, TAX EVASION

The notion of 'tax avoidance' (and 'anti-avoidance') is a consistent source of sometimes heated debate, both legal and extra-legal (the emergence of tax avoidance both as a social evil and as the target of a distinct legal norm is discussed in chapter five). A pithy one-line definition of 'tax avoidance' is possible without being glib: a taxable person engages in tax avoidance when they do something to prevent a tax obligation (in whole or in part) from arising at all, or to defer it, in a manner which was not intended by the legislature. To take advantage of the tax allowance or relief in a manner intended by Parliament is not 'tax avoidance' but mere 'mitigation'. In *IRC v Willoughby* [1997] STC 995, Lord Nolan said at 1003:

> The hallmark of tax avoidance is that the taxpayer reduces his liability to tax without incurring the economic consequences that Parliament intended to be suffered by any taxpayer qualifying for such reduction in his tax liability. The hallmark of tax mitigation, on the other hand, is that the taxpayer takes advantage of a fiscally attractive option afforded to him by the tax legislation, and genuinely suffers the economic consequences that Parliament intended to be suffered by those taking advantage of the option

Of course, ascertaining whether Parliament 'intends' that a particular allowance or relief be available to a particular taxable person who undertakes a particular taxable activity will not always be a straightforward exercise. To put monies into a statutorily exempt savings fund is 'mitigation'. Parliament has invited (perhaps positively encouraged) taxable persons to do this. Conversely, to export an asset abroad and re-import it to attract tax relief available to 'imports' may well be 'tax avoidance': it is likely that the legislature did not intend import reliefs to be given to assets exported and re-acquired just to obtain the reliefs. There will be transactions the characterisation of which will not be at all (so) clear-cut.

The identification of Parliament's intention (or supposed indifference to a tax avoidance objective) is the very battleground of avoidance cases. It may become a sterile exercise: one person's 'mitigation' is another's 'avoidance'. In other words, the definition of 'tax avoidance' begs the question 'how do you know what was or was not the intention of Parliament?' And while the answer is 'interrogation of the relevant taxing provisions' and the process of statutory construction of the relevant provisions can at least take a proper shape once the legislative objective of these provisions is identified, value laden terms as 'mitigation' and 'avoidance' are necessarily imprecise and to that extent rob the law of predictability and consistency (more of this in chapter five).

Quite different to tax avoidance is 'tax evasion': a person engages in 'tax evasion' when they seek to escape payment of an existing tax obligation, which is a criminal act: *IRC v Challenge Corp Ltd* [1986] STC 548, 555 (per Lord Templeman). To simply under-declare trading receipts is 'tax evasion'.

8. THE MODEL APPLIED TO SOME UK TAXES

Saying something is so does not make it so. The model presented above is generic. While it uses examples from income tax, it claims to hold true for all taxes. To test this claim, it is useful to map the model onto some seemingly uncontroversial 'taxes' (all of the 'taxes' considered here are discussed in standard works: see Loutzenhiser 2022).

The UK tax code imposes UK-wide taxes in a series of primary Acts of Parliament. This locates those taxes firmly within the province of public law imposed by a Parliament with a continuing absolute sovereignty. The devolved Parliaments within the UK have certain tax-raising powers which are not discussed in this work. His Majesty's Commissioners of Revenue and Customs ('HMRC', an arm of the executive) generally administer the collection and enforcement of taxes in the UK: The Commissioners for Revenue and Customs Act 2005, section 5.

For non-corporate persons, ITTOIA 2005 has provisions which tax the following putative taxable activities: trades (ITTOIA 2005, Part 2), property (investment) income (ITTOIA 2005, Part 3, which has rules for both a 'UK property business' and an 'overseas property business'), other investment income (interest and dividends) (ITTOIA 2005, Part 4), income from intellectual property (ITTOIA 2005, Part 5,

Chapters 1–4) and income which, although not in law one of these types of income, is sufficiently close in nature for the draftsperson to think that this income should be taxable in the hands of a 'taxable person' (if there is one) (ITTOIA 2005, Chapter 8; for example, commission payments where the payee was not conducting a trade: *Ryall v Hoare* [1923] 8 TC 521). Employment income is taxed under the Income Tax (Earnings and Pensions) Act 2003 (ITEPA 2003).

These taxes are all uncontroversially 'income taxes'. Each of these activities has its own set of rules which define a 'taxable' person, define the 'tax' base to compute a 'taxable' amount by applying a 'tax' rate and impose 'tax' compliance and enforcement provisions. All the taxable amounts for each taxable activity are computed for a taxable person's income tax computation and then aggregated to yield a single 'taxable amount'. It is this taxable amount which is subjected to a tax rate to produce the income tax payable by the taxable person. IHT and VAT have their own separate computations and tax rates.

There is a parallel regime for the taxation of UK tax resident companies in the Corporation Tax Act 2009 (CTA 2009) and the Corporation Tax Act 2010 (CTA 2010), which statutes also contain special additional provisions such as those which concern the taxation of corporate debt (CTA 2009, Part 5) and intellectual property ('intangibles': CTA 2009, Part 8).

All of these taxes follow the basic structure of the model described in this chapter. The model is now applied to income tax on trades, CGT, IHT and VAT.

INCOME TAX ON TRADES

(1) *Taxable person.* For trading profits, a 'taxable person' is a person who receives or is entitled to the profits of a trade (generally, the trader, but also a beneficiary with an 'interest in possession' in a trust where the trustees are trading) *and* is either 'UK resident' or, if that person is 'non-UK resident' carries in a trade wholly or partly 'in the UK': ITTOIA 2005, sections 6, 8. Thus the 'putative taxable activity' is the carrying on of a 'trade' and the additional connecting factors are (1) an entitlement to the profits of a trade and (2) 'UK residence' or, for 'non-UK residents', the carrying on of a trade at least partly 'in' the UK.

'Trade' is notoriously difficult to define. Statute does not help. The case law is vast and nuanced. There are many borderline cases and the border itself is imprecisely crawn in the case law. Very broadly, a 'trade' is the sale of goods or services to a customer where the profits are obtained by more than simply exploiting rights of ownership. In other words, the profit is more than just the realisation of capital appreciation of the value of any goods sold and any income return is not simply the function of ownership rights (for example the receipt of rents from property owned by the recipient which they have let out). For goods, the recipient has engaged in some commercial activity to generate the profit beyond simply owning goods and realising their value. This additional activity would turn the realisation of an 'investment' into 'trading stock'. For example, if a person who does not have a property dealing business acquires a holiday home and later sells it, any profit is very firmly a function of ownership. But if that person demolishes the holiday home and erects a two-story office block, the profit of sale reflects something more than mere ownership and is likely to be a trading profit: *Lynch v Edmondson* (1998) Sp C 164; *Marson v Morton* [1986] 1 WLR 1343.

Tax 'residence' in the UK is now defined by reference to the statutory residence test in Finance Act 2013, Schedule 45. This refers to a mixture of physical factors, such as the number of days present in the UK, the attributes of the person whose residence is being tested, such as whether they have a home in the UK and whether they work full time outside the UK, and their 'ties' to the UK, being family, accommodation, country or work. Thus, a person who is neither UK tax resident nor carries on a trade in the UK is a not taxable person and no UK income tax on trading income can arise at all.

(2) *Tax base*. The definition and computation of the profits of a 'trade' are done on a year-by-year ('tax year') basis, usually using generally accepted accounting practice, which will, for each tax year, throw up a profit or a loss: ITTOIA 2005, sections 24, 25; the equivalent corporation tax provisions are CTA 2009, sections 46, 47. Statute often modifies the accounting measure of trading profits. For example, an accounting measure of profit will deduct many expenses, whereas the UK tax code only permits the deduction of those expenses which are incurred 'wholly and exclusively for the purposes of [the trade]', so an accounting deduction will not necessarily give rise to a deduction for the purposes of income tax. This is a harsh test: black clothes worn to comply with professional

rules in court do not satisfy this test, as clothes are also worn for 'warmth and decency' and thus cannot be said to be acquired 'wholly and exclusively' for the purposes of a barrister's profession: *Mallalieu v Drummond* [1983] STC 665.

(3) *Taxable amount and tax rates*. All sources of chargeable income are combined with the taxpayer's marginal rate applying to the aggregate of their chargeable income (ITA 2007, section 23); thus, marginal rates apply and increase as profits increase. The rates of tax are the basic rate, higher rate and additional rate: ITA 2007, section 6. These are set by Parliament each tax year. The basic rate of 20 per cent applies to the first £37,000 of chargeable income, the higher rate applies to chargeable income above that except that the additional rate of 45 per cent applies to taxable income over £125,140: ITA 2007, section 23, applying the rates announced in the Spring 2023 Budget. Each taxpayer is provisionally entitled to a personal allowance (at the time of writing, the personal allowance is £12,750 and is frozen until 2028/29: ITA 2007, section 35(1); Finance Act 2021, section 5(2) as amended by Finance Act 2023, section 5(3)) but that entitlement is progressively reduced (by 50 pence for every pound earned over £100,000) as the taxpayer's earnings increase: ITA 2007, section 35(2)–(3). Note, also, that this computation is logically downstream from the assessment of whether there is a taxable person.

(4) *Compliance and enforcement*. A taxable person (here the person carrying on the trade and receiving or entitled to the trade profits who is either UK resident or, if non-UK resident, carries on a trade wholly or partly in the UK) must give HMRC notice of his chargeability to income tax (Taxes Management Act 1970 (TMA 1970), section 7) and, if given a notice to do so, make a 'self-assessment' (that is, a self-computed return) of trading profits each year (TMA 1970, section 8). If HMRC dispute the computation of the tax, this dispute is ultimately settled in litigation in the regime established in the Tribunals Courts and Enforcement Act 2007. Tax debts are money debts due to the Crown and enforced as such: TMA 1970, sections 67 and 68 (which apply to certain specified taxes but are generally imported in statutes which impose other taxes). The mechanics of enforcement do not affect the proposition that it is Parliament, not the 'Crown', which, through legislation, imposes taxation at central government level.

Income tax on trades thus conforms to the model set out above.

CAPITAL GAINS TAX

(1) *Taxable person.* A person is a taxable person if they 'dispose' of 'assets' (any form of property except sterling currency: TCGA 1992, section 21(1)) *and* are either UK resident (TCGA 1992, section 2(1); there are also temporary non-residence provisions designed to keep short-term emigrants as taxable persons, charging them to CGT on gains made during their absence upon their return: see TCGA 1992, section 1M) *or*, if non-UK resident, dispose of a UK situate asset used for the purposes of a branch or agency through which the non-UK resident carries on a trade, profession or vocation: TCGA 1992, sections 1A, 1B.

There are special rules for assets which comprise UK land and assets which derive at least 75 per cent of their value from UK land: TCGA 1992, section 1C. So the putative taxable activity is the disposal of an asset (wherever situate for a UK resident or UK situate for a non-UK resident). The additional connecting factors are those of (1) UK residence, (2) conduct of a trade, profession or vocation through a branch or agency in the UK for a non-UK resident or (3) the disposal of land (or assets deriving at least 75 per cent of their value therefrom) situated in the UK.

(2) *The tax base.* The taxable receipts are the consideration received on a disposal (TCGA 1992, section 21) (or, where the asset is disposed of otherwise than by way of a bargain made at arm's length, the market value of the asset: TCGA 1992, section 17) in any year of assessment. The permitted deductions are any monies expended wholly and exclusively to acquire the asset, any monies expended to enhance the value of the asset (so long as that enhancement is reflected in the state and nature of the asset at the time of disposal) and incidental costs of disposal: TCGA 1992, section 38. All taxpayers are entitled to an annual exemption which is currently £6,000: TCGA 1992, section 1K. Special rules apply to non-UK domiciled persons who dispose of non-UK situs assets (TCGA 1992, section 275). There are also rules which attribute specific statutory deductions, such as a deemed market value acquisition cost for assets acquired on death (TCGA 1992, section 62).

(3) *Tax rates.* From 6 April 2019, the rate of CGT is dependent on the type of person making the disposal and the type of asset which is the subject of the disposal: TCGA 1992, section 1H. The rules are complex, but broadly

chargeable gains by an individual are charged at 10 per cent or 20 per cent (TCGA 1992, section 1H(3), depending on the unused basic rate band: see above) subject to reliefs, such as business asset disposal relief (TCGA 1992, section 169K, in which case the gain is charged at 10 per cent). Gains in the hands of trustees are charged at 20 per cent (subject, again, to the exception that a rate of 10 per cent applies to disposals qualifying for business asset disposal relief). There are special rates for the disposal of residential property: such a disposal by a trustee is always charged at 28 per cent (TCGA 1992, section 1H(7)), and by an individual is charged at 18 per cent or 28 per cent depending on whether there is any remaining unused basic rate band based on the individual's taxable income (TCGA 1992, section 1H(2)).

(4) *Compliance and enforcement*: A taxable person must self-assess chargeable gains in broadly the same way as for income tax on trading profit: TMA 1970, sections 7–8. As with assessments of income tax, HMRC can raise assessments or amend self-assessment returns within certain time limits.

So capital gains tax, too, instantiates the juristic model of taxation set out above.

INHERITANCE TAX

(1) *Taxable person.* All non-corporate persons are within the charge to IHT. There is no exclusion for any person, wherever resident. The putative taxable activity is the disposal of an asset (which may be an actual disposal or a deemed disposal, such as on death) which reduces the value of the transferor's 'estate': IHTA 1984, sections 3–5. A charge to IHT, then, is measured by what is given away ('a transfer of value'), not what is received. IHT is a disincentive on gifts, whether during life, or on death. While, at first sight, no further connecting factors are required for a person to be a 'taxable person', this is misleading, as an examination of the IHT tax base reveals.

(2) *The tax base.* It is the tax base which confines the charge to IHT to events with a UK connection. IHT is charged on an amount which is a 'transfer of value' (the amount a person gives away): IHTA 1984, section 3. This amount is the amount by which a person's 'estate' (that which they

beneficially own) is diminished by a gift. But the estate of an individual who is non-UK domiciled (and who is not treated, by IHTA 1984, section 267 as being UK-domiciled) does not include property not situated in the UK. Such property is 'excluded property' by virtue of IHTA 1984, section 6. So the putative taxable activity is the making (deemed or otherwise) of a relevant transfer of value and the additional connecting factors are (1) domicile of the taxable person in a part of the UK; and (2) the relevant assets being situated in the UK. Put another way, the attributes of the transferor (their domicile) affect the scope of a charge to IHT, which means that domicile is properly viewed as a connecting factor attributable to the status of a person as a taxable person (not the tax base).

(3) *Taxable amount and tax rate.* Immediately chargeable lifetime transfers are taxed at a minimum of 20 per cent: the rate is liable to increase if an individual dies within seven years of the transfer: IHTA 1984, section 7. Certain transfers ('potentially exempt transfers' or 'PETs') may never be taxed if made more than seven years from the transferor's death, but transfers are otherwise taxable at a maximum of 40 per cent (with tapered relief available if made within seven years of the transferor's death): IHTA 1984, section 3A. A transfer of value on death is generally taxed at 40 per cent (a possible reduction to 36 per cent applies where charitable donations of at least 10 per cent of the taxable estate have been made): IHTA 1984, section 7. Agricultural and business property reliefs of 100 per cent are available where the relevant conditions are met: IHTA 1984, Part V, Chapters 1 and 2. Transfers between spouses are exempt: IHTA 1984, section 18. All individuals also have the benefit of a nil-rate band, which at the time of writing, is £325,000: IHTA 1984, section 7 and Schedule 1.

(4) *Compliance and enforcement*: A taxable person must report transfers of value: IHTA 1984, section 216. Where HMRC consider that there has been a transfer of value, they can give 'notice of a determination' to any person who they consider to be liable for IHT: IHTA 1984, section 221.

So IHT also conforms to the model set out above; and the existence of a taxable person is chronologically prior to the other steps, albeit that the all-important connecting factors, domicile and situs, are revealed by the provisions concerning the computation of the tax base.

VALUE ADDED TAX

VAT was first introduced by reason of the UK's obligations as an EU Member State but has survived Brexit and remains part of the UK tax code in the Value Added Tax Act 1994 (VATA 1994).

(1) *Taxable person.* A taxable person is one who makes a 'supply' of goods or services and has registered for VAT: VATA 1994, section 4. Registration is either voluntary (any UK-established person carrying on a business and/or making taxable supplies can register: VATA 1994, Schedule 1, paragraphs 9(a) and (b)) or compulsory (where the turnover (not profit) of a UK-established person has exceeded a specified amount or there are reasonable grounds to believe that it will exceed the prescribed registration limit within the following 30 days, which at the time of writing is £85,000 in the previous year (assessed on a rolling monthly basis): VATA 1994, Schedule 1, paragraph 1). Further, supplies are taxable if made 'in' the UK (VATA 1994, section 4) and the person is 'UK established' (has a fixed place of business in the UK) (VATA 1994, Schedule 1). Thus the putative taxable activity is the making of supplies of goods or services by a person registered for VAT. The additional connecting factors are the need for supplies to be made 'in' the UK and for the person to be 'UK established'.

(2) *The tax base.* VAT is imposed on the taxable person's turnover on such supplies ('taxable supplies') and is known as 'output VAT': VATA 1994, section 24(2). Should the taxable person have to pay VAT on supplies made to them for the purposes of making taxable supplies, the taxable person may deduct that VAT paid from the VAT due as 'input tax': VATA 1994, sections 24–25.

(3) *Tax rate.* the basic rate on taxable supplies is generally 20 per cent (VATA 1994, section 2) although a varied rate of 25 per cent applies to supplies of certain antiques and pieces of art (VATA 1994, section 21(4)). Reduced rates apply to certain supplies; indeed there is a category of 'zero rate' supplies where there is no output tax at all but the taxable person may recover payment of input tax: VATA, section 30, Schedule 8.

(4) *Compliance and enforcement.* HMRC have conduct of the administration of VAT. Persons registered for VAT are required to make quarterly (or, occasionally, monthly) VAT returns reporting the value of turnover

from taxable supplies in the relevant period: VATA 1992, Schedule 11, paragraph 2(1); VAT Regulations 1995 (SI 1995/2518), regulation 25A. HMRC are permitted to challenge those returns and raise further assessments within certain time limits: VATA 1994, section 77. VAT is a debt due to the Crown: VATA 1994, Schedule 11, paragraph 5(1).

VAT therefore also instantiates the model set out above, illustrating that it is a model which is apt to encompass both direct and indirect taxes.

9. FINAL THOUGHTS ON THE MODEL

The provisions which treat a tax obligation as a debt to the Crown do not, for any tax, establish any trust (statutory or otherwise) over any part of a taxable person's property (certainly not over their pre-tax receipts), which means that the money debt is non-proprietorial. The important implications of this feature of the UK tax code and of taxation generally are explored in chapter three.

What this brief survey of the specific taxes within the UK tax code (not just income tax but other taxes such as IHT and VAT: the claim is that the model holds good for all taxes) discussed here demonstrates is that the model is an accurate description of taxes. These taxes are different in nature. Income tax on trades taxes self-employed persons, whereas income tax on employment receipts taxes employees. Income tax (whether for self-employed or employed persons), CGT and VAT all tax amounts received, whereas IHT taxes amounts given away. Income tax, CGT and IHT are all direct taxes: there is an assumption that the person on whom the formal incidence falls (the taxable person) will bear the burden of the tax. VAT is an indirect tax. The assumption is that the final consumer of the goods and services sold will bear that burden (but note the taxable person is the seller). More fundamentally, the model shows that for these very real taxes, if there is no taxable person, there is no further tax analysis to be done (even in the case of IHT, where primacy is given to the tax base, the domicile of a person matters as to the taxability of certain gifts).

Thus the model described in this chapter incorporates key ideas *within* tax law (taxable person, tax base and taxable amount, tax rate and tax compliance and enforcement obligations, together with the parasitic but still key ideas set out above), makes good the foundational nature of the notion of a 'taxable person' (which is critical for all UK taxes except IHT when it comes to distinguishing taxes from other money obligations in chapter four) and the personal, non-proprietorial nature of a tax obligation (which is critical when it comes to assessing the juristic nature of a tax obligation and its consequences in chapters three and six). Moreover, it illustrates that taxation can be understood purely through the lens of its juristic features, and so need not (indeed must not) be defined in terms of its purposes, which, as chapter two shows, are many and varied. This chapter makes these features of a tax charge clear not only as a matter of abstract analysis but also in the context of actual tax provisions of the UK tax code.

RESPONSE TO CHAPTER ONE

JONATHAN PEACOCK KC, 11 NEW SQUARE (CHAIR OF THE REVENUE BAR ASSOCIATION 2013–16)

In tax law, like many other areas of the law, the simplest questions are often the hardest to answer. And it is surprising just how often those simple questions arise in practice and go on to trouble the Courts. The model set out in this chapter brings intellectual rigour and order to the very building blocks of any modern tax code and sets out how we might better understand what it is that makes a charge a 'tax' rather than some kind of levy, impost or fine. Moreover, once that question is addressed we can proceed to test the relevant nexus between a taxable person and/or a jurisdiction and different types of taxable economic activity, thereby founding the tax charge in a particular location and helping to set the tax base. This in turn allows higher level classification – often relevant when it is the very nature of a tax which is being challenged – as a 'direct' or 'indirect' tax; or some feature of a tax as being a 'relief' or an 'exemption', the philosophical difference being between 'subject to tax but with the burden relieved' and 'not subject to the burden at all'; or what it means to 'avoid' a tax.

Now, a sceptical reader might wonder how important such conceptual matters are in practice. The reality is that questions of this sort are quite common, as can be seen from a couple of examples.

(1) In 2001 the UK Parliament introduced a new, environmentally focused, tax on the extraction of 'aggregates' (stone, sand, clay and the like) in the UK. This tax was challenged by operators in the industry on the basis, inter alia, that the tax was a 'direct tax' which was not permitted under EU law or that the various 'exemptions' from the tax were so incoherent that the resulting system amounted to unlawful 'state aid' (again contrary to EU law), being unwarranted incentives or disincentives on those who extract different types of aggregate. While both charges were rejected (see *British Aggregates Associates v HM Treasury* [2002] EWHC 926 (Admin)) the Court was forced to grapple with both the issue of what made a charge a 'tax' properly so-called and the nature of that tax in the context of a new type of impost.

(2) The UK CGT code levies tax on capital gains made on the disposal
     of most types of assets. In some circumstances the gain inherent in
     one asset can be deferred (and in effect 'rolled over') into the gain on
     another asset where the former is swapped for the latter and there is
     no 'tax avoidance' motive. If a UK-based taxpayer swaps one asset,
     pregnant with gain, for another without charge to CGT and then
     leaves the UK before selling the second asset, has he engaged in tax
     'avoidance' by leaving the jurisdiction in which the charge would
     be imposed? While there is a perfectly reasonable argument that he
     has not, since (to anticipate chapter five) leaving the jurisdiction
     which imposes the tax charge does not thereby defeat the intention
     of Parliament, the courts proceed on the basis that putting oneself
     outside the ambit of a 'tax' can (or, indeed, does) amount to 'avoid-
     ing' the tax: see *Snell v HMRC* [2007] STC 1279.

In this way it can be seen, I hope, that this chapter is, in many respects, the
most important in this work. One cannot proceed to the more difficult,
and sometimes more interesting higher-level questions, without a proper
understanding of the relevant building blocks.

*Author's response: Mr Peacock's response highlights how a definitional
exercise is conceptually critical. It also illustrates the application of the
model to not only direct taxes, such as income tax and CGT but also to EU
law and aggregates taxes, which is a welcome illustration of the scope of the
relevance of the model.*

2

Modal, Not Functional

Law (including tax law) is a mode, not a function. Law is a means (mode) of pursuing one or more objectives, all of which might be achieved (whether more or less effectively) by other means. Law cannot be defined by reference to one or more of the functions it serves. So 'law' is not defined as '*the* means of regulating human behaviour'. Rather, law is one of a number of means of regulating human behaviour; see Gardner 2014, 293 (emphasis added):

> [L]aw is not a functional kind. It is a modal kind. There is no social function, nor any combination of social functions, that distinguishes law from any of its near neighbours [such as morality, or religion] … [L]aw is distinguished from many of its near neighbours … by *how* it serves the many social functions that it, in common with those near neighbours, serves or is capable of serving.

This observation has implications for how tax law is properly approached.

1. THE TAX CHARGE MODEL AS A VEHICLE FOR LEGAL, SOCIAL AND POLITICAL NORMS

It is obvious that the key ideas within tax law described in chapter one may be informed by any number of legal, social and political norms, which may well change over time. The UK tax code is an obvious vehicle for communicating political ideas (and ideology) from the legislature to the governed.

For example, in relation to who are taxable persons, a non-UK resident is not a taxable person on non-UK source trading income or non-UK source interest because the UK respects public international law (at least in this context). A charity is not a taxable person for CGT to encourage charitable activity. In relation to the tax base, tax neutral transfers between spouses (TCGA 1992, section 58) were extended to civil partnerships, reflecting a change of both legal and social norms. Business and agricultural property (but not family homes) are privileged for IHT purposes in that a transfer of value of such property is reduced, so that a parent may transfer their valuable family company to their children free of IHT (or, in certain cases, at reduced rates) but a parent cannot transfer a family home to a child without attracting IHT.

As discussed above, tax rates (flat, proportionate and progressive) have very different impacts on taxable persons depending on their wealth. Imposing VAT (or any other indirect tax) at a flat rate on goods and services will impose a greater relative cost on the less wealthy than would imposing proportionate or progressive rates of income tax (to take £1 from a person who has £10 imposes a greater burden on that person than to take £1 from another person who has £100).

Sometimes the UK tax code is slow to repeal outdated norms. For example, the rule that a wife's property (both income receipts and proceeds from the disposal of investment assets) belonged to her husband for tax purposes (so that the husband alone was taxed at his marginal rate) was expressly repealed only with effect from 1990: FA 1988, section 104.

Tax law is also used as a tool for promoting change in public attitudes and behaviour. Modern examples include: the soft drinks industry levy ('SDIL' or 'sugar tax') introduced from April 2018 to tackle perceived a perceived cause of obesity; increases in excise duty on the import of cigarettes to discourage smoking; and the 'cycle to work scheme' (to allow employers to provide bicycles and/or safety equipment to employees in certain circumstances without that provision constituting a taxable benefit in kind: ITEPA 2003, section 244); which may encourage physical exercise and a modal shift from the use of cars which would be consistent with achieving climate change objectives.

2. THE VARIOUS OBJECTIVES OF TAX LAW

In principle, tax law can pursue a variety of social functions, with no common connecting factor amongst any these objectives.

CITIZENSHIP OBJECTIVES: TAXATION AS A CONDITION OF SUFFRAGE?

Although taxation is not, in the UK, imposed as a condition of suffrage, there is no structural reason why it should not be. Mill argues (Mill 1861b, 174):

> The assembly that votes the taxes, either general or local, should be elected exclusively by those who pay something towards the taxes imposed. Those who pay no taxes, disposing by their votes of other people's money, have every motive to be lavish and none to economise … He who cannot by his own labour suffice for his own support, has no claim to the privilege of helping himself to the money of others.

Mill further thought that the exclusion of illiterate and innumerate from the suffrage guaranteed competence, the suffrage being restricted to those 'being able to read, write and … perform the common operations of arithmetic'.

A tax liability is not a condition of suffrage in any part of the UK. And there are fundamental objections to Mill's view. First, even on its own terms, the beneficiaries of expenditure have an interest to ensure those benefits continue and are not exhausted by 'lavish' tendencies in spending policy. Second, Mill assumes those with the most expertise are those who are taxed. This is not at all obvious. Inherited wealth and (taxable) wealth generated from activities which are commercially fruitful but intellectually undemanding are two examples of sources of taxation and taxable persons who do not necessarily have any expertise in public financing and expenditure. Third, it is unlikely that those in need of benefit will pay substantial amounts of tax, so Mill's approach results in a structural disconnect between the contributors to a fund and the fund's beneficiaries. But the theoretical prospect of taxation as a surrogate for a political voice remains.

CITIZENSHIP OBJECTIVES: A FORM OF JOINT ENTERPRISE

In a separate description of taxation as a function of citizenship, the imposition of a tax liability has been judicially described as the function of a form of joint project between the citizen and the State, along the lines of what Oakeshott would term an 'enterprise association': Oakeshott 1975, 200–03. An enterprise association, in Oakeshott's world, is 'a relationship [between citizen and state where both have a shared goal] from which an agent may extricate himself by a choice of his own', as opposed to a 'civil' association, which has no common substantive purpose other than the cementing of intra-population loyalties, a civil association being governed by 'non-instrumental' rules: Oakeshott 1999, 137.

In *Wankie Colliery Co Ltd v IRC* [1922] 2 AC 51, Lord Sumner said at 69: 'The excess profits duty imposed under Finance (No 2) Act 1915, during the First World War] ... appears to be due to the State's desire not to penalise the profiteer, but to *participate in the fortuitous prosperity of a time of war*' (emphasis added). The reference to 'participation' connotes some sort of mutual endeavour of taxpayer and State. But the notion of 'participation' as an explanation of taxation is not useful, since it serves as a blanket description of the more specific objectives that taxation may seek to achieve, discussed below. It is to these other objectives of taxation to which we now turn.

OTHER (NON-CITIZENSHIP) OBJECTIVES OF TAXATION

Having looked at functions which taxation could, but does not, have in the UK tax code, taxation may pursue one or more of the following objectives. The description of these bases is not original: see Loutzenhiser 2022. However, the analysis of the distinct objectives sought by the respective bases and the different notions of justice which underpin them are those of the writer alone, as are their implications for a juristic definition of taxation.

These non-citizenship functions are, if not always mutually exclusive, distinct from one another.

(1) *Finance of public goods.* First, taxation effects an allocation of resources ('public goods'): Murphy and Nagel 2002, 76. This 'public-private division' determines how much of a society's resources will come under the control of government and how much is left in the discretionary control of private individuals. Public goods include the minimal conditions considered necessary for society to exist at all, such as domestic peace and

security. Such 'public goods' cannot be provided to anybody unless they are provided to everybody. The important point to bear in mind is that once a particular good is identified as a 'public good', which the market could not function without, its funding by taxation is the funding of a *necessity*. As to what properly constitutes a 'necessity', that is a matter of debate which is outside the scope of this work.

Here taxation is a *quid pro quo* for 'services [which taxpaying citizens] cannot dispense with or even, if [they] wished, refuse': Simmel 2004. 'Services' does not mean supplies made to a consumer. 'Services' here means those functions which are necessary for a society to be able to function such as courts, an army, and so on: financing these is an act of self-preservation. This basis for taxation would encompass the 'benefits' accruing to resident and non-resident taxpayers inherent in the connecting factors of residence and source. However, the role of taxation as a mechanism for the finance of 'public' goods is not synonymous with discredited 'benefits' theories of taxation, whereby taxation is a payment for state 'benefits', the logic of those theories would have the greatest beneficiaries of such State 'benefits' (and thus most likely the poorest) paying the greatest tax, absent unconvincing arguments as to the value of the 'benefits' being greater to the rich than to the poor (see, for example, Mill 1861b). For a summary of such 'benefits' theories, see Cooper 1994.

(2) *Redistribution.* Second, taxation may fulfil a redistributive function, in allocating wealth (however defined) in varying proportions amongst different individuals: Simmel 2004. Redistribution may have several conceptions. All human beings have worth and claims. Distributive justice looks 'to aim at equality and to favour the needy to reduce inequality': Raphael 2001, 5. For example, governments may assume a responsibility to mitigate harm to certain market participants who lose out in the operation of that marketplace (or individuals who are unable for whatever reason to participate in the marketplace). Taxation may serve to implement 'economic and social background justice', for example to maintain the Rawlsian difference principle: Rawls 2001. (See ibid, 160–62, for Rawls' consideration of the different types of taxes (estates tax, progressive income tax, proportional expenditure tax) best suited to achieve these ends.) To confine government responsibility (and taxation) to the funding of public goods is, for some, 'just too minimal': Rawls 2001, 181, 182. Redistribution may alternatively seek to reconcile the freedom to spend and the injustice of good luck inheritance (Dworkin

2002, 347, 348), or to avoid a concentration of wealth (Duff 2017, 167, 186, 168; Bird-Pollan 2017, 217, 224), or to encourage experimentation (Fleischer 2017, 260, 285).

(3) *Social engineering*. Third, taxation may be employed as a tool of social engineering (distinct from redistributive justice). So, taxation may be used as an incentive; for example, interest arising on certain statutorily approved 'savings certificates' (broadly representing borrowings by or approved by the Treasury) is exempted from tax, to encourage investment in such certificates: see ITTOIA 2005, section 692. Or taxation may be used as a disincentive. Thus, taxation may be imposed to increase the price of alcoholic drinks with the objective of restricting consumption for health reasons: see Case 333/14 *Scotch Whisky Association and Ors v The Lord Advocate and The Advocate General for Scotland*, [42]–[50] of the judgment of the Court.

(4) *Economic management*. Fourth, taxation may be used as a tool of economic management, say, to dampen demand (Friedman and Heller 1969) or, conversely, to incentivise investment in a particular geographical area (see, for example, Capital Allowances Act 2001, section 45K – tax relief for expenditure on plant and machinery on specified 'designated assisted areas').

(5) *Finance of commercial activities which are not public goods*. Fifth, taxation may finance the government's engaging in commercial activities, either in competition with the private sector or as a monopoly (such as telecommunications): *Executive Aircraft Consulting Inc v City of Newton* 845 P 2d 57 (Kan 1993).

Here taxation *either* performs a commercial role, supplementing government revenues to enable certain services to be provided (but does not amount to anything that is or is analogous to private law consideration for those services, since taxpayers may include those to whom the services are *not* provided), *or* it works to perform a redistributive goal by enabling people to access beneficial services that they could not procure by private means. This form of redistribution could be seen as an instance of 'rotational justice', where the interests of all are catered for by having certain activities funded through taxation whether or not particular taxpayers benefit from those activities or not: see Feinberg 2003. Alternatively, it can be seen as a form of (value-pluralistic) perfectionism: '[There is] no fundamental principled inhibition on governments acting for any valid moral reason', so that government may promote the good life, by means, inter alia, of taxation: Raz 1989, 1232; see also Raz 1986, 415.

Whether a particular tax helps to fund the provision of a 'public good' as opposed to raising finance to promote 'non-public good' governmental activities is controversial and not easy to establish, an observation made starkly obvious by the privatisation of services such as the delivery of utilities such as transport, water, gas or telecommunications, so that certain services which were once perceived as public goods are now relegated to the status of services which may be consumed (and paid for by consumers) or not.

OBJECTIVES NEED NOT BE CONNECTED

These various objectives that taxation might pursue are clearly distinct and may be indeed contradictory. Some objectives may imply maximising revenue, whereas others are neutral or indeed interested to minimise revenue, by disincentivising the taxable activity. Payment for public goods (and the finance of government-provided, non-public goods) seeks to maximise aggregate taxation to secure the conferral of those goods. The redistribution objective would equally involve seeking to maximise monies raised from the wealthy. An incentive given by a tax reduction relating to the taxable activity may either reduce the aggregate tax take or increase it if a larger number of persons take up the taxable activity being incentivised. Tax as a disincentive positively aims for lower or no tax revenue arising from the disincentivised activity if the disincentive is successful (or at least a very high tax revenue if the disincentive is unsuccessful).

It is wholly unsurprising to find a jurist describing taxation as a 'sort of legal maid of all work ... serving a multitude of obscure ends': Fuller 1964, 166. Fuller provides a rare acknowledgement of the multiplicity of the objectives sought by tax law:

> Taxes have been imposed to control the business cycle, to identify professional gamblers, to allocate economic resources, to discourage the use of alcohol, to make vendors of cosmetics share with the government a part of the high price women are willing to pay for their unnatural beauty, to discourage travel, to expand federal possibilities and who knows for what other objectives? (166)

Less generously, tax law has been described as 'a 'black box' technology that can be called upon to distribute economic benefits and burdens without the need to consider the internal properties of the black box itself': Hamlin 2018, 18.

OBJECTIVES MAY BE ACHIEVED BY OTHER MEANS

Further, each of these functional objectives may be served by alternative means, legal and non-legal. Alternative legal means may be identified which might (more or less effectively) achieve each of the objectives attributed to taxation.

Any number of criteria may be appropriate to identify conditions for suffrage, none of which are taxation (place of birth, economic ties, long term residence etc). A joint enterprise between citizen and State may be achieved through other compulsory commitment mechanisms, such as compulsory purchase of citizens' property, or conscription. Public goods (and other government goods and services) could be funded or secured through the compulsory acquisition of resources (say the compulsory acquisition of property to build a motorway, or courthouse). The same is true of redistribution, in that property, rather than money, may be compulsorily acquired for redistribution. Incentives may be conferred by, say, the free provision of goods and services and disincentives may be effected through the criminal law, rather than through taxation.

This point is important. That a particular legal mechanism has the same objective and the same effect as a tax does not make it a tax. So a legislature or executive with delegated powers are free to adopt a mode of extraction (say compulsory purchase) which is not a 'tax' but raises money in exactly the same way (and for exactly the same purpose) as a tax would have done. This is what shows the modality of law and the modality of tax law in particular in action.

Taxation's modal nature is thus very clear indeed. And while nevertheless taxation is a single, coherent body of law, with distinct characteristics, as demonstrated in both chapter one (which establishes taxation's generic model) and chapter four (which shows how tax law is distinct from other monetary obligations), taxation's modal nature has important consequences which are explored in this chapter.

3. IMPLICATIONS OF TAXATION'S MODAL NATURE

NO ABSOLUTE 'GOOD' OR 'BAD' TAX

The modal nature of taxation, whereby taxation has distinct functions which a particular tax might seek to fulfil, exposes the fallacy of any absolutist notion of a 'good' tax structure. Adam Smith's famous 'Canons of Taxation' (see Smith 1776, Book 5, Chapter 2, 825–28) suggest that taxation should be charged in proportion to ability, should be certain and not arbitrary, should be charged at the most convenient time to the taxpayer, whilst minimising compliance and collection costs.

While these principles are intuitively consistent with a view of taxation as a means of finance (whether of public goods or not), since the relevant finance is raised with minimised costs to both taxpayer and tax collector (and the certainty of a prospective tax charge is rule of law compliant), they do not hold across the pursuit of all objectives. For example, taxation employed as a tool of economic management, especially as a disincentive (including for social objectives, like as a brake on alcohol consumption), is (at its lowest) indifferent to any inconvenience to taxable persons and might well be quantified without any reference to ability to pay. The fact that a tax directed at reducing alcohol consumption makes it more difficult to buy alcohol is the very point of the tax.

The same is true of other attributes of a so-called 'good' tax structure, such as its effect on economic incentives, fairness amongst taxpayers and resource allocation amongst different sectors of society: see the report of the Meade Committee 1978, 20 as updated in the analysis of the Mirrlees Review (Adam 2011, 22). The same observation means that 'neutrality' is not a feature which all 'good' tax structures should aspire to (as suggested by Smith 2015, 102–03). A disincentive or deterrent in the mode of a tax charge is properly indifferent to 'fairness' amongst taxpayers measured in terms of sacrifice of taxpayers' resources. Even rule of law notions such as certainty and predictability may yield to stronger and more immediate (legitimate) concern. For example, retrospective legislation may be proper to raise money for an immediate and pressing emergency, such as war, or a health emergency.

Of course, principles of fairness may dictate that all the canons of taxation hold good for a particular tax, despite taxation's modal nature, but the point made here is that they cannot derive uncontested validity in each and every case from any single function sought to be achieved by taxation: see the Mirrlees Review for a modern analysis of a 'good' tax system and its key principles of a coherent relationship to a benefits system, neutrality and progressivity which is a nuanced and penetrative study of tax law from the perspective of an economist's objectives for taxation.

STATUTORY INTERPRETATION SHOULD RESPECT TAXATION'S MODAL NATURE

The modal nature of tax law means that when construing the text of relevant statutory provisions (that is, those which define a taxable person, identify the tax base, apply a tax rate to a taxable amount and impose tax compliance and enforcement obligations), the function that the particular tax provision seeks to fulfil should be borne in mind. Because taxation is modal, a single approach to the construction of tax statutes is misconceived. The following best describes the correct approach to the construction of a statutory provision:

(1) *Text*. Ascertain the (objective) meaning of the text of the provision: '[A]n objective assessment of the meaning which a reasonable legislature as a body would be seeking to convey in using the statutory words which are being considered': *R (Project for the Recognition of Children as British Citizens) v Secretary of State for the Home Department* [2023] AC 255 ('*PRCBC*'), at [31] (per Lord Hodge). The text is the obvious and primary signal of legislative direction, on the basis that a citizen is entitled to rely on what they read: ibid at [29] (per Lord Hodge).

And separately, when considering proposed legislation, given compressed legislative timetables, Members of Parliament must be able to rely on the ordinary meaning of the words: Sales 2019, 54–55. The reasonable legislature assumes that circumstances change over time and that a statute will apply to those changed circumstances and this justifies the 'always speaking' doctrine, which accommodates prevailing social attitudes and norms and developing scientific knowledge at the time when the statute is being interpreted even if those have changed since the time of enactment.

For example, the construction of the statutory grounds on which it is unreasonable for a spouse to be expected to continue to live with the other spouse are very different in 2018 to those of, say, 40 years previous: *Owens v Owens* [2018] AC 899. This doctrine requires 'taking into account changes in our understanding of the natural world, technological changes, changes in social standards and, of particular importance here, changes in social attitudes': *Owens* [2017] EWCA Civ 182, at [31] (per Sir James Munby P).

Thus the meaning of a statutory text is informed by both extra-legal norms and legal norms. Extra-legal norms may arise from social attitudes. Legal norms may arise not only from specific legislative acts but by implication from the legal background which also changes over the years. The legal structure relating to equal treatment, now highly visible in the Equality Act 2010, means that what is or is not legally acceptable behaviour is very different to what this was in 1970, before the enactment of the Sex Discrimination Act 1975 and the Race Relations Act 1976.

Both extra-legal and legal norms may be accommodated by way of the always speaking doctrine relatively easily where the statute uses broad value-laden terms such as 'reasonable'. Alternatively, changing attitudes (or indeed, simply the correct reading of statutory provisions in principle, see below) may be accommodated by reading words into statutory provisions. Sometimes the language may be altered by substitution, though this is permissible only to cure drafting mistakes, where the court is 'abundantly clear' both that Parliament failed to properly enact a discernible purpose and what the substance of a correctly drafted provision would have been (*Inco Europe Ltd v First Choice Distributions* [2000] 1 WLR 858). It follows that a court cannot, under the guise of construction, distort the express words of a statutory provision (*O'Rourke v Binks* [1992] STC 703, at 710 (per Scott LJ)). Furthermore, the notion of 'drafting error' suggests that only a drafting error made at the time of enactment entitles a court to read words into a statute. This approach may, however, have been extended by *UBS AG v HMRC* [2016] STC 934: see further chapter five (on tax avoidance's reprehensibility as a legal norm).

(2) *Principle.* In selecting one of several possible candidate linguistic meanings, identify the meaning which accords best with 'principle', meaning the textual meaning which is most consistent with:

    (a) The legislative context, which encompasses (i) any relevant statutory definition, (ii) the relevant term within the relevant provision, (iii) the relevant provision within the relevant fasciculus of provisions, (iv) the relevant provision within the relevant statute more generally and (v) the relevant statute within any wider statutory framework of legislation dealing with the same subject matter; and

    (b) Parliament's (the 'reasonable legislature's') (imputed) intention in enacting the relevant provision: 'It is the duty of the court, in accordance with ordinary principles of statutory interpretation, to favour an interpretation of legislation which gives effect to its purpose rather than defeating it': *Test Claimants in the FII Group Litigation v HMRC* [2022] AC 1, at [155] (per Lords Reed and Hodge).

(3) *Authority.* Of course, case law may, for lower courts, provide a binding answer to the meaning of a term but the exercise of identifying the correct meaning in principle at stage (2) will not only help to distinguish cases with precision but also help any court not bound by relevant authority (the UK Supreme Court) and arbitrators who are often not bound by authority to follow decisions they consider to be wrong in principle.

This process is not a sterile formulaic approach. The battleground of 'principle' at stage (2) is an interrogation of legislative intent, legal coherence and the meshing of legal technique and evolving social attitudes. This exercise of ascertaining the correct meaning 'in principle' of a word may well involve a sophisticated scrutiny of legal and extra-legal norms. The archaeology of the process of statutory construction presented here ensures that the text of the relevant provision not only represents the correct starting point but imposes linguistic limits on this process.

    The process is captured in the House of Lords' direction to construe the relevant statutory provision 'purposively' and apply that purposive construction to the facts 'viewed realistically': *Barclays Mercantile Business Finance Ltd v Mawson* [2005] STC 1 at [36]–[38]. 'Purposive' construction is a synonym for stage (2). This exercise is as true for tax statutes as for any other statutes. A tax provision designed to raise monies for public goods is completely different in its objective from a tax provision

designed to disincentivise alcohol consumption. That they are both juristically 'tax provisions' means that they share the same legal archaeology
(they both fit into the model set out in chapter one, if the money obligation is imposed on a 'taxable person' who has specific tax-connecting
factors to the taxing authority). But they need not be construed the same
way.

Thus, in principle, a charge to tax to fund public goods, without
which society could not exist or function, need not (indeed ought not) to
be construed restrictively. Once it is appreciated that there is no correlative link between liability to taxation and property rights, the justification
for a restrictive construction falls away. On the contrary, a restrictive
construction of a tax charge with the sole purpose of funding public
goods (assuming such a charge exists) would seem to be *in tension* with
the requirement that the courts should give effect to Parliament's intention. If 'public goods' are those goods necessary for a society to survive,
this last observation is not exceptionable.

Different considerations apply to the extent that taxation seeks to
fulfil objectives beyond those solely concerned with the provision of
public goods, such as the redistribution of resources, since the personal
monetary liability which is imposed reflects a particular political agenda
(assuming redistribution to be distinct from the conferral of a public
good). In such cases, the width or narrowness of the relevant provisions
which ultimately impose a charge to taxation will reflect political choices,
so as to yield the greater or lesser exposure to tax liability for redistributive purposes.

As for taxation used as a mode to implement social incentives or disincentives, or as a tool of economic management, Parliamentary intention
should inform the scope of the relevant liability to taxation; this, too,
may require a broad or narrow construction, depending on the nature
of the policy pursued. Finally, in relation to taxation to fund government
activities, Parliamentary intention should also inform the construction and application of the relevant statutory provisions, in the light of
the general law which governs private law contracts, procurements and
competition law.

The modal nature of the law of taxation militates, therefore, against
a single approach to the construction of all tax provisions. Such an
approach would give conclusive importance to the nature of taxation
(a personal monetary liability) and ignore entirely the modal nature
(diverse purposes) of taxation. However, tax provisions historically have

been construed and applied in a generic way, on the basis that all 'tax provisions' (in contra-distinction to other statutory provisions) must have the same approach taken to them.

In *News Corp UK and Ireland Ltd v HMRC* [2023] UKSC 7, the Supreme Court had to decide whether the term 'newspaper' extended to digital forms of news (and was thus entitled to a favourable 'zero-rate' VAT treatment (see chapter one) for the purposes of VATA 1994, Schedule 8, Group 3, Item 2), where the digital form was materially identical to the printed edition. Lords Hamblen and Burrows (with whom Lords Hodge and Kitchin agreed), delivering the leading judgment of the court, held 'no' on the basis that the textual term 'newspaper' was restricted to printed matter, even in the light of the 'always speaking' doctrine. Lord Leggatt provided a concurring but separate analysis, discussed below, which interrogated the 'always speaking' doctrine and adopted the generic approach to tax provisions criticised in this chapter, ignoring the clear legislative purpose of the relevant provisions.

So far as Lord Burrows and Lord Hamblen were concerned, statutory context was key. A 'standstill' provision restricted the favourable VAT treatment to items within its scope as at December 1975, when digital forms of news were not contemplated. The statutory context accordingly prohibited an updated meaning of 'newspaper'. This is an example of Stage 2(a) of the interpretative exercise set out above (that is, in accordance with principle as a matter of statutory context) in action. While the standstill provision was consistent with some development, one of the policies underpinning the preservation of existing zero-rated categories was the prevention of social hardship that might result from abolishing existing exemptions. Because that policy could not be engaged by digital newspapers (there having been no access to digital editions at the material time), the court was justified in adopting a construction which excluded such publications. Although the social policy behind the legislative decision to zero-rate printed newspapers was the promotion of literacy, the dissemination of knowledge and democratic accountability by having informed public debate (*News Corp* [13]) and this policy would have been served by extending the zero rate to digital newspapers, this was irrelevant given the other considerations just referred to. The approach taken by the majority thus considered that the text and the immediate objective of the statute were sufficiently clear to prevail over the more general objectives behind zero rating newspapers. Lord Hamblen and Lord Burrows thus displayed a sensitivity to the need for interrogation of the specific provision demanded by tax's modal nature (*News Corp* [46]):

> [T]he fact that the same social purpose may be served by zero-rating two related items does not mean that they should or will be treated the same way. Taxation involves budgetary and political decision-making and how far to extend exemptions from tax is a budgetary choice. Such decisions are made on a granular basis.

The approach of Lord Leggatt was different. Lord Leggatt concurred with the conclusion in the leading judgment, but did so on the basis that the 'always speaking' doctrine should properly distinguish between (i) altering a statutory meaning to reflect changes over time (which amounted to impermissible 'legislation' by judges) (*News Corp* [88]) and (ii) applying an unchanged meaning to new (albeit uncontemplated) circumstances (which is a permissible, indeed unavoidable, incident of the interpretive process) (*News Corp* [90]–[92]). To treat the word 'newspapers' as covering digital editions would fall into the latter category, giving it a new meaning.

For Lord Leggatt, the term 'newspaper' could accommodate a digital edition as a matter of language, but the statutory context of zero-rating (a tax relief) meant that the term had to be construed strictly because tax is a money-raising mechanism and thus any tax provision, including zero-rating, must be construed strictly (*News Corp* [105]). It was the nature of tax as a money-raising mechanism, not the standstill provision, which Lord Leggatt prayed in aid to restrict the meaning of 'newspaper'. Whilst Lord Leggatt's judgment was couched in terms of a general principle that derogations from the basic aims of a statute are to be interpreted narrowly, his focus on the basic aims of 'a taxing Act' effectively treated tax as generically functional (to raise revenue) and neglected not only the modal nature of tax itself but also ignored the nature and purpose of the relevant provision (to promote democratic accountability).

(Incidentally, neither Lords Burrows and Hamblen on the one hand, nor Lord Leggatt on the other, appealed to a specific presumption in VAT that exemptions ought to be construed strictly (which would have attracted further analysis of whether zero-rating provisions are properly considered as 'exemptions').)

The generic approach adopted by Lord Leggatt is mistaken. It assumes that all tax provisions have the same objective, which is

incorrect. Further, the approach adopted by Lord Leggatt cuts the term
'newspaper' from its legislative context and applies a different set of
criteria, focused on porous distinctions drawn between different vari-
eties of linguistic change. In particular, Lord Leggatt's omission to
engage with the purposes of the standstill provision overlooked both
Stage 2(a) (the broader statutory context) and 2(b) (the intentions
of a reasonable legislature). This approach confuses means and ends.
Parliament sought to give a privileged status to 'newspapers' for good
reason. The 'always speaking' doctrine would (but for the standstill
provision) have accommodated Parliament's objective by extending this privilege to digital forms. That Parliament sought to do this
by extending a favourable tax treatment is, in a sense, a mechanistic
detail. To frustrate Parliament's intention by looking at the nature of
the mechanism which Parliament used rather than Parliament's objective is wrong in principle. By contrast, the appeal of the majority to
the standstill provision is an unexceptionable reliance on Parliament's
express intention, as expressed in that provision, to inform the limits
of the provision.

The narrow point that *News Corp* illustrates is therefore that the
modal nature of tax prohibits the formulaic application of interpretive presumptions, including the presumptions that derogations from
the basic purpose of a statute are to be interpreted narrowly. The wider
lesson is that the modal nature of tax law means that purely functional
approaches to the construction of tax statutes, and especially those that
attribute a generic purpose to all tax statutes, will generate errors. In
order to understand the meaning of a given provision, it is always necessary to follow the three-stage interpretive approach outlined above (text,
principle, and authority) in respect of that particular provision.

Nevertheless, the generic approach to construction is pervasive.
There is much dicta that equates all taxation to a criminal sanction and
commits to a generic 'literalist' construction: '[Taxation is] … kindred
to the creation of a penalty or the establishment of a crime' (*Ormond
Investment Company Limited v Betts* [1928] 13 TC 400, 426 (per Lord
Buckmaster)). An extreme formulation of this approach is formulated in
Rowlatt J's observation in *Cape Brandy Syndicate v IRC* [1921] 1 AC 64,
at 71, that

> In a taxing Act one has to look merely at what is clearly said. There is no room
> for intendment. There is no equity about a tax. There is no presumption as

to a tax. Nothing is to be read in, nothing is to be implied. One can only look fairly at the language used.

This is mistaken: there is no basis for such an analogy to crime for any tax, let alone all taxes (and see chapter four as to why taxation is completely distinct from a criminal fine). Neither is this criticism an unfair revisitation of early twentieth-century attitudes through a twenty-first-century purposive lens. Tax was never analogous to a criminal fine. And most words are capable of having more than one meaning, so to exclude 'intendment' in favour of a narrow construction, where an alternative tenable construction, even if less common but more consistent with Parliament's intention, is wrong in principle.

It does not follow that a requirement for 'clear' or 'plain' legislative authority (because tax is somehow analogous to a penalty or criminal sanction) justifies a literalist approach. Even less so an approach which disregards purpose. Whether there is a 'clear' or 'plain' legislative power to impose a monetary imposition upon a person within a legislative (or indeed common law) jurisdiction of a putative creditor is answered by reference to the available relevant admissible legal material. But this is not restricted to the words of a particular legislative provision, in the case of statute, viewed in isolation. '[T]he question is whether, on an informed interpretation of the enactment, there is no real doubt that the grammatical interpretation is that intended by the legislator. It is not whether the enactment, *read literally*, contains a plain meaning' (Bailey and Norbury 2020 ('*Bennion*'), 441).

That the purpose of an enactment is itself a component of the legal material (howsoever legitimately gleaned) has been acknowledged for a very long time. Viscount Simonds said in *Attorney-General v Prince of Hanover* [1957] 1 WLR 436, at 460–61:

> I conceive it to be my right and duty to examine every word of a statute in its context, and I use 'context' in its widest sense ... including not only other enacting provisions of the same statute, but its preamble, the existing state of the law, other statutes in pari materia, and the mischief which I can, by those and other legitimate means, discern the statute was intended to remedy.

Thus, the necessity for the imposition of a tax to be authorised by statute does not import any mandatory literalist approach to construction. Indeed, any commitment to a strong literalist approach to the construction of all tax statutes, as an amorphous class of statutes in particular, has been expressly rejected. See, for example, the seminal observations of Lord Steyn in *IRC v McGuckian* [1997] 1 WLR 991, at 999–1000:

> tax law remained remarkably resistant to … new non-formalist methods of interpretation. It was said that the taxpayer was entitled to stand on a literal construction of the words used regardless of the purpose of the statute … Tax law was by and large left behind as some island of literal interpretation … [and although in *Ramsay (WT) Limited v IRC* [1982] AC 300, Lord Wilberforce] restated the principle of statutory construction that a subject is only to be taxed upon clear words[, to] the question 'What are "clear words"?' he gave the answer that the court is not confined to a literal interpretation [but rather] … 'There may be, indeed should, be considered the context and scheme of the relevant Act as a whole, and its purpose may, indeed should, be regarded'.

Examples from case law of statutory provisions being construed *contra proferentem* against a tax authority are located in antiquity. The authorities cited in *Bennion* (at 729) for the proposition that 'there are many cases where the court has refused to adopt a construction of a taxing Act which would impose liability where doubt exists' were decided a very long time ago: *Tomkins v Ashby* (1827) 6 B&C 541 at 542 (stamp duty not to be charged unless the intention is plain); *Micklethwaite* (1855) 11 Exch 452 at 456 (subject not to be taxed without clear words); *Partington v Attorney-General* (1869) LR 4 HL 100, at 122 (equitable construction not admissible in a taxing statute); *Oriental Bank Corporation v Wright* (1880) 5 App Cas 842 at 856 (clear and unambiguous language necessary to impose a tax charge).

Nevertheless, the notion seemingly persists that tax legislation should be construed without regard to the particular purpose of a particular provision (that is, without regard to the acknowledgement that taxation is a legal mode which could serve any one of a variety of purposes). So, for example, it is said that tax legislation (that is 'tax legislation' generally) has been subjected to a literalist approach by those who favour a 'small state' approach (that is, presumably, where the reach of a state-tax collecting authority's power is confined to its narrowest terms), whereas a more expansive approach to the construction and application of taxing provisions betrays a commitment to a larger state (and hence an acceptance of a more purposive and expansive construction and application of taxing provisions). Snape 2017 considers that

> It is easy to argue for a literal approach if you believe in minimal government, abhor administrative discretion and are zealously loyal to the foundational

principle of representative consent to taxation. The purposive approach, however, demands a judicial viewpoint that accepts the need for a large government, the inevitability of administrative discretion and a pragmatic loyalty to representative consent.

There are two criticisms that come to mind. First, the political views and objectives of a judge (by contrast to the legislature) cannot properly inform how statutes are to be construed without offending the separation of powers. Second, if the suggestion here is that a literalist approach is generally to be regarded as minimising the scope and ability of a taxing authority to impose and collect tax, whereas a purposive or expansive approach is to be properly viewed as yielding a greater statutory legitimacy for imposing and collecting tax, it is simply wrong. Unpacked, the small state approach presumably calls for a narrow approach to the definition of a taxable person and to charging provisions but not necessarily for relieving provisions which reduce a taxable amount, unless the very relief exhibited a large state approach and required a narrow constriction to confine its effect.

As for a connection between consent to taxation and construction, if Parliament's intention is to impose a tax, a narrow construction to frustrate this intention is illegitimate: there is nothing in a purposive approach that dilutes 'consent' to a 'pragmatic' consent. In any event, this approach does not reflect case law. As long ago as 1962, in *IRC v R Woolf & Co (Rubber) Limited* [1962] Ch 35 (at 44–45), the company law definition of a 'member' of a company was rejected for the purposes of the Income Tax Act 1952, section 255(2), to attract a charge to surtax on a lending banker. Thus, a purposive construction yielded less tax, not more. And as recently as in 2017, in *X-Wind Power Limited v HMRC* [2017] UKUT 0290 (TCC), the Upper Tribunal held that the inadvertent submission of an Enterprise Investment Scheme (EIS) compliance statement, prior to the submission of an Seed Enterprise Investment Scheme (SEIS) relief claim, for the purposes of the Income Tax Act 2007, section 257EE, precluded the company's investors from claiming SEIS relief, despite the fact that the company intended to make a compliance statement for SEIS and the use of the wrong form was 'attributable to an inadvertent and innocent mistake' (at [6]). On a literal reading of the relevant provisions, the Upper Tribunal held that the submission of the EIS compliance certificate was fatal to the claim for SEIS. Thus, a literal construction led to more tax being payable, not less.

A blanket literal approach to interpretation is unjustified in both principle and authority. The instrumental justification explored in the preceding paragraph rests on a false assumption about the respective effects of literal and purposive approaches. The purpose and context of a statutory provision are powerfully relevant to its meaning. This is vividly illustrated by *News Corp*, discussed above. Lord Leggatt was right to acknowledge that the meaning of a contested term like 'newspapers' was not discernible by reference to the ordinary meaning of the words, and that consideration of the provisions' purposes was paramount. Where Lord Leggatt erred, as with judicial approaches to the interpretation of tax statutes more broadly, was in adopting a monist, functional conception of 'tax'. The modal nature of taxation requires a heterogeneous, provision-specific approach to the construction of tax statutes.

That is not to say that a general legislative intent is never appropriate. General presumptions against retrospectivity, or, as will be seen in the discussion in chapter six, the legal norm that tax avoidance is reprehensible have their place. What is crucial is that the invocation of general legislative intent does not obscure the fact that statutes and the provisions within them may serve more than one goal. Where multiple relevant purposes are discerned, the weight to be accorded to each will be an interpretive question to be analysed within the three-stage framework set out above.

The explanation for the seemingly persistent approach to treat all tax provisions the same, irrespective of the modal nature of taxation, may well lie in the misconceived perception that there is a relationship between a liability for taxation and a property obligation. For example, *Bennion* suggests (at paragraph [27.6]) that:

> interference with property may take many forms. All kinds of taxation involve detrimental property rights or other economic interests. So do many criminal penalties, such as fines, compensation orders and costs orders. Compulsory purchase, trade regulations and restrictions, import controls, forced redistribution on divorce or death, and maintenance orders are further categories.

The next chapter shows that taxation does not impose a property obligation. And such an approach deprives the interpretation of tax provisions of its necessarily modal nature, approaching the issue instead negatively, solely by reference to its supposed effect on property rights.

SUMMARY

This first key idea about tax, taxation's modality, shows that (1) there are no such things as generic 'good tax' attributes as a matter of legal principle (the Mirrlees Review of course has a lot to say about when a particular tax is well designed to achieve the economic objective it seeks) and (2) tax provisions should not be subjected to a 'one-size fits all' interpretive approach (but acknowledges that case law often adopts such an approach). Each tax provision ought to be construed in its own specific legislative context, not subjected to generic assumptions. This may not be saying much but in the light of the contrary approach of much of the case law discussed in this chapter, it is saying quite a lot.

RESPONSES TO CHAPTER TWO

SIR JONATHAN RICHARDS, JUSTICE OF THE HIGH COURT OF ENGLAND AND WALES

Until recently, I imagined myself to be 'good with computers'. I can usually get my computer to perform the limited range of tasks I request of it. I am to be found shaking my head in bewilderment at the screen less frequently than some other judges. That all changed a few weeks ago, when I removed the back of my computer to replace the hard disk. The bewildering array of circuitry made me realise that I had a limited perspective that came entirely from time spent in front of the screen and keyboard. Mr Ghosh KC's stimulating chapter has invoked similar feelings about tax. For quite a few years now, my perspective on tax law has been that of a judge sitting at the front of the court and listening to parties making an argument on its application. I have therefore used tax law to determine a series of unrelated disputes. I have seldom had cause to consider the complicated circuitry that lies behind the mechanism as a whole and am grateful to Mr Ghosh for broadening my perspective.

Given my perspective on tax law, I am intrigued by Mr Ghosh's suggestion that the modal nature of tax could require different approaches to the construction of different types of tax provision. I see the force of the intellectual argument that a tax to fund 'public goods' should not be construed restrictively. However, how is the judge in the courtroom to know whether a particular tax is of this character or not? No doubt a government that invites Parliament to enact a new tax will argue strongly that it is funding 'public goods' such as the court system and the defence of the nation. However, the government's political opponents may have a different perspective, arguing that the tax in question is simply an enabler of waste and mismanagement of the public finances. In a similar vein, a government might say that a particular tax is intended to affect citizens' behaviour by, for example, deterring them from consuming as much alcohol. The government's political opponents might say otherwise, claiming that, just as the income tax charge on profits of a trade is not intended to deter trading activity, so a tax on alcohol consumption is intended to raise revenue from alcohol consumption, rather than to act as a disincentive to alcohol being consumed. How is a judge to know whose perspective is correct without considering matters of politics or policy that are often thought to be outside a judge's remit? Might the answer change over time depending on whether alcohol consumption declines while the tax is in place?

I mention these points not to cast doubt on Mr Ghosh's typically thought-provoking analysis but rather to highlight what seems to me to be an important aspect of tax's modal nature, at least in the United Kingdom. Modal though it is, tax law pursues its objectives in a specific manner, which involves disputes as to its applicability in particular cases being settled by a tribunal independent of the government of any particular day, of Parliament and of officials at HM Revenue & Customs. I would suggest that an analysis of the consequences of tax's modal nature should bear that feature in mind. If that is correct, then even if tax's modal nature means that there are no well-defined criteria for describing a tax as 'good' or 'bad', it might nevertheless be said that a tax is 'bad' in particular circumstances. If, with the objective of deterring consumption of fatty foods, Parliament enacted a tax requiring anyone consuming such foods to pay 'such amount of tax HM Revenue & Customs consider just and reasonable in the circumstances', I would suggest that the tax can fairly be described as 'bad'. That is not because of the objective that it pursues, but rather because disputes about it could not be resolved by the kind of independent tribunal that tax law's modal nature envisages.

Author's response: Sir Jonathan's response highlights the difficulty of ascertaining the purpose of a particular provision (this comes with the territory of being a lawyer, whether counsel or a judge), which in turn puts pressure on the influence of taxation's modality on statutory construction. No argument there. But this does not result in a 'default position' of so-called 'literalist' construction, let alone a single, generic default position. More fundamentally, Sir Jonathan reflects on what amounts to rule of law concerns in relation to statutory construction (for example, allowing HMRC to have discretion on the imposition of tax), which are very real. So, for example, a submission that anti-avoidance provisions should be construed broadly so that uncertainty of application is a form of deterrence, has been described by the Supreme Court as 'improper': HMRC v Fisher [2023] UKSC 55 at [76], Lady Rose. The reader is invited to consider when such rule of law concerns act as a sort of 'tie-breaker' to prefer one construction of a provision over another or when (if ever) such rule of law concerns are properly normatively trumped by Parliamentary sovereignty which gives HMRC wide discretion.

PROFESSOR JAMES PENNER, NATIONAL UNIVERSITY OF SINGAPORE

Identifying taxation as a *modal* as opposed to a *functional* kind is the most important theoretical aspect of taxation that any student of the subject must grasp. On the distinction between 'modal' and 'functional', the basic idea is simple. Consider getting the kids to school in the morning. The purpose, or function, of what one does is to get the kids to school. Any way of doing this fulfils the function of getting the kids to school. These ways are 'means' or 'modes' of doing so. Driving the kids in the car is one means or mode. Walking them to school is another. But, of course, driving somewhere or walking somewhere is a multi-purpose or multi-functional means or mode of *doing something else*, achieving one's purpose, here, of getting the kids to school.

With respect to the law itself, it has no essential purposes or functions. The law can regulate, or at least try to regulate, any human behaviour. This is not to say that it should, of course. But the point is that the law is a certain kind of social technique involving the promulgation of rules, adjudicating conflicts, with legislative and adjudicative officials there to make this particular mode or means operate effectively. But this means is obviously capable of achieving any number of functions, whether criminalising some behaviour, regulating the distribution of a person's property on their death, protecting consumers from exploitation and so on and so on.

As Ghosh explains with admirable clarity, the same is true of the particular legal mode of taxation, by which any kind of activity (which can encompass what might be called 'passive' activities, such as receiving dividends on shares) can be made the subject of a *tax charge*, the nature of which is explained in chapter one. But imposing a tax charge may serve any number of purposes, or ends, or functions. It may be imposed to raise revenue to fund public goods. Or it may be imposed to discourage an activity without directly regulating or prohibiting it, as with the case of what are sometimes called 'sin taxes', on alcohol or tobacco consumption or gambling. The whole point of such taxes is not to raise revenue because, if successful, the tax will raise little revenue if any. A third obvious purpose of imposing a tax charge is to steer the economy in one direction or another, by raising or lowering (in the case of tax reliefs) the costs of particular economic activities.

These insights are obscured by the prevalent idea that taxation has a specific purpose or function: to raise revenue for the provision of public goods. The thought is not untoward – much of the law of taxation has exactly this purpose. But as Ghosh instructs us, adopting this prevalent view has two serious deleterious consequences.

The first is that it suggests that any tax as such can be judged good or bad by the same criteria. It might well be true that a tax whose function is simply to raise revenue for the provision of public goods should not be 'distortionary', that is, cause taxpayers to make economic decisions they otherwise would not have made, thus interfering in the allocative function of markets. But that cannot be true of 'sin taxes' or taxes whose very purpose is to steer the economy in one direction or another, for example, by encouraging the development of green energy and discouraging the use of fossil fuels. In short, whether a tax is a good or bad tax can only be *relative* to the particular function the tax is aiming to achieve.

The second serious consequence concerns the construction of taxing statutes: treating taxation as a functional kind – the function of generating revenue for the provision of public goods – as an across-the-board interpretive strategy cannot but lead to the ignoring of the *particular* function any taxing statute aims to achieve, which will in turn lead, inevitably, to thwarting Parliament's intentions in any number of cases.

Author's response: Professor Penner's response makes visible the important theoretical point that law is modal, so each area of law has a presumptive modal nature which may (although not in the case of tax law) be confined to achieving a very particular objective. For example, property law has clear specific inherent objectives of providing, to a greater or lesser extent, rights of exclusion and rights to deal. Tax law, for the reasons given in this chapter, retains a general modal character which necessarily informs how particular tax provisions ought to be construed.

3

Personal, Not Proprietary

As was observed in chapter one, the taxes discussed there all impose a tax charge which is a non-proprietary debt owed to the Crown and while a tax charge may impose a proprietary debt, there is no example of such a tax in the UK (tithes are discussed separately below). Such a non-proprietary obligation is an obligation to deliver money to the taxing authority. So long as the taxable person finds and pays sufficient monies to satisfy their tax obligation, the taxing authority is necessarily indifferent to where that money comes from (the taxable person's own resources, or the taxpayer's rich aunt). References to money obligations and to debts in this chapter are to non-proprietorial debts because tax charges in the UK are exclusively debts of this type.

A personal obligation to deliver money for a non-proprietorial debt (which a tax obligation is) is not a property obligation over any particular property. This obvious proposition has been ignored in most analyses of tax law, certainly by philosophers. However, the distinction is critical for both jurists and philosophers.

1. THE INDIVIDUATION OF PROPERTY AND PERSONAL RIGHTS AND OBLIGATIONS

The distinction between personal and property rights and obligations depends upon the class of persons against whom remedies lie. According to Birks (2005, 28), the question is 'against whom can rights be demanded?' So the 'personal' or 'property' nature of a particular right identifies the class of persons who owe a particular duty to a particular person by reason of duty imposing norms. If a creditor can enforce a debt only against the debtor and not against the world in relation to an item of the debtor's property, the debtor's obligation is a personal one.

PROPERTY RIGHTS

A property right is a 'real right', being 'a right in or over an identifiable asset or fund of assets': Goode and McKendrick 2010, 28. Such a real right can be generally asserted against third parties and survives the bankruptcy of the obligor. Such real rights are 'good against the world' and 'multital': Hohfeld 1978.

PERSONAL RIGHTS

By contrast, Roy Goode (2010, 30) notes that a purely personal right is

> one which does not involve the delivery or transfer to the obligor of an identified asset or funds of assets but is to be satisfied by the obligor's personal performance in some other way, such as the payment of a debt or damages from his general assets.

The distinction is between 'what I *own* and what I *am owed*': Goode 1987; Goode and McKendrick 2010, 30–31. Personal rights are thus 'only good against the obligor' and 'paucital': Hohfeld 1978, 69–74.

PROPERTY OR REAL RIGHTS: CORRELATIVE OBLIGATION IN REM

A real property right in rem in an identifiable asset entails a correlative duty in rem, that is, a duty which relates to the identifiable asset in which the right in rem is held. This is often expressed as a duty of non-interference, which correlates to the right-holder's right to exclude others from enjoyment of the right-holder's property.

PERSONAL RIGHTS: CORRELATIVE OBLIGATION OR DUTY IN PERSONAM

A duty/obligation to perform personal services as the correlative liability to a personal right is not attached to any *asset*. Indeed, it is the personal performance of services for the obligor which may be enforced.

This is obvious for, say, obligations owed by an employee to work under a contract for services. It is equally true for a money-debtor.

2. THE INDIVIDUATION OF MONEY DEBTS

Creditor rights are 'property' rights but debtor obligations are personal obligations (and not property obligations). Simply put, a creditor may well describe their rights as a form of 'property': choses in action that – depending on their terms – may be assigned and turned to account by the creditor. But these creditor's rights do not give the creditor a property right in any particular property of the debtor, whose obligation to the creditor is personal. Money debts yield an asymmetry where a creditor's rights are a form of 'property' (which is a separate identifiable asset that the creditor owns) but the debtor's obligation to pay is a 'personal' obligation only. However, philosophers have often confused them, certainly in the context of taxation (see chapter six).

DEBTS

A money debt is a 'mere right [of a creditor] to demand payment of money [from the debtor] at a stipulated time': Bell 1870. Examination of the respective rights of creditor and debtor reveals that money debts may well give rise to a 'property' right of the creditor but that the debtor's correlative obligations for a non-proprietary debt are not 'property' obligations.

CREDITOR'S RIGHTS WHICH ARE A RIGHT IN REM

It is possible for a creditor to have a right 'in rem' in a debtor's asset (here termed 'proprietary debts'). In English law a defendant's wrongful disposition of a claimant's property may attract a claim to the proceeds of sale in the hands of the defendant as the beneficiary of a constructive or automatic resulting trust. But tax obligations are not proprietary debts (being simply debts owed to the Crown in money, nothing more: see chapter one).

DEBTOR'S OBLIGATION UNDER A MONEY DEBT IS NOT A 'PROPERTY' OBLIGATION

A non-proprietary debt, where a debtor's obligation is confined to paying a sum of money to a creditor, is not a property obligation, even though the creditor may describe their rights as 'property'. The debtor may continue to exercise all their rights of excludability (and transfer-ability, where solvent) in respect of all their assets in the face of their debt-obligation. Money may, of course, be the subject of property rights, which may be owned and transferred. But the creditor's claim does not attach to any specific item of property (including money) owned by the debtor. Where a creditor has no rights in rem as regards specific assets of a debtor, there is no property obligation on the part of the debtor.

Equally, the debtor's inability to pay does not absolve them from the debt: *Universal Corp v Five Ways Properties Ltd* [1978] 3 All ER 1131. The debtor may fund payment of the debt by any means, for example by means of a gift received from a relative, so there is no connection between a debtor's property and their obligations at all. The creditor, for a personal debt, never had rights in the debtor's property. It is in this asymmetric sense that it has been observed that '[t]he right to be paid is a property right, and thus legitimately falls within the law of property, and the obligation to pay forms part of the law of obligations': Tarrant 2011, 688.

The nature of rights in security, even those rights which are rights in rem, for example, security over English real property or Scots heritage, does not undermine this analysis. Such rights, although exigible against specific items of property, are distinct from (and their exercise contin-gent on) a failure by the debtor to satisfy their personal obligation to pay the money debt, which is the primary obligation.

3. TAXATION AS A DEBTOR'S MONETARY OBLIGATION

The obligation of a taxable person to pay their tax is a money obligation (chapter one), which is thus a personal obligation and not a property obligation. It is against this critical notion of a tax liability as a monetary obligation that the anatomy of a charge to tax must be viewed. The identification of a taxable person and the computation of a tax obligation from a tax base (having applied the relevant tax rate) gives rise to a monetary liability for the person subject to the relevant provisions.

It is also convenient to observe at this stage that, although a tax liability must be paid in money, a tax liability is payable irrespective of whether a taxpayer has sufficient monetary assets to meet that liability. Not only might the tax base yield a taxable amount (say by reference to the application of deeming provisions which treat, for example, a non-arm's length transaction to be made at market value, whatever the actual consideration (if any) may be: see TCGA 1992, section 17), so that the liability itself is computed without the need for the taxpayer to have received money in a particular transaction, but even if a taxpayer has spent his receipts, the tax liability remains, of course, payable.

Furthermore, there is no provision in the UK tax code which requires a taxable person to pay tax out of their own resources (see chapter one: the debt due to the Crown does not create any obligation to pay tax out of particular funds). As with an obligation to pay money, it is a liability to deliver money, whether funded by one's own resources, or borrowed or, indeed, gifted from another. This has implications for the effectiveness of taxation in particular modes, discussed below.

THE NATURE OF A TAX AUTHORITY'S RIGHTS

It is useful to examine a tax authority's rights which are co-relative to a taxable person's tax obligation, both as a cross-check against the personal, non-property obligation of the taxable person and as a worthwhile exercise in its own right.

The monetary nature of a tax liability as indistinguishable from other money debts is confirmed by a brief consideration of the creditor's rights in respect of a tax liability, which demonstrates (contrary to Markby 1996, 93–94 and Raz 1980, 31–32) that a tax creditor does indeed have property rights in a tax claim, in contra-distinction to the purely personal monetary obligation of a taxpayer-debtor. However, just as for money debts generally, these property rights subsist in the debt itself which is owned by the creditor, not in any asset owned by the debtor. This analysis also reinforces the conclusions in chapter five that taxation need not be paid to a public body.

Markby concludes that a tax creditor has no rights because the power to collect the tax is effectively at the absolute will of the tax collector (Markby 1996). This ignores the separation of powers. In the context of the UK tax code, the duty to pay taxes is not established or created by HMRC but is rather in the hands of the legislator (Parliament). There is no absence of a 'right' on the part of a creditor as the correlative of a taxpayer's duty to pay taxes, such as would distinguish a tax debt from any other type of monetary debt.

The property nature of a tax creditor's right to collect the money due from a taxpayer is made even clearer when the prospect of *assignment* of that right is contemplated. From the perspective of a taxpayer who has a creditor's right to repayment of tax, it is clear that a taxpayer is entitled to assign its claim for repayment of VAT: *Midlands Co-Operative Society Ltd v The Commissioners of HMRC* [2008] EWCA Civ 305. The notion that a tax imposing body might assign the right to payment of a tax liability is not fanciful. The practice of tax farming, where the state leases or assigns to a private individual the right to collect taxes typically in return for fixed periodical payments, has been adopted in various historical contexts, including ancient Rome and *Ancien Regime* France.

In the contemporary United States, the Internal Revenue Service (IRS) has assigned its right to collection of certain overdue federal tax debts to four private contractors who have the power to collect, on the government's behalf, outstanding inactive tax receivables. This was authorised under a federal law enacted by Congress in December 2015; section 32102 of the Fixing America's Surface Transportation Act (FAST Act) requires the IRS to use private collection agencies for the collection of outstanding inactive tax receivables. In the UK it is not possible at present for HMRC to assign any right of tax collection without further legislative authority, since the TMA 1970 requires payment of taxes within its scope to be paid to HMRC. But there is no constitutional principle which would prevent Parliament from enacting a statutory regime like that of the United States to permit such an assignment. The result would be that tax monies would be payable to non-public bodies (with no statutory power to raise taxes). This is relevant when we come to consider some standard definitions of 'taxation' in chapter four, which confine the notion of taxation to monies raised by or payable to public bodies.

A tax liability does not create any trust in favour of HMRC. So, a taxpayer may do what he chooses with monies representing a tax liability. For example, in *Attorney-General v Antoine* 31 TC 213 the taxpayer used, without any legal impediment, monies representing an amount that should have been paid to satisfy a PAYE liability (per Croom-Johnson J at 219). This point has been consistently endorsed: 'Money collected as [VAT], though expressly added to the invoice as [VAT], is not thereby impressed with any trust in favour of the Commissioners' (*In re John Willment (Ashford) Ltd* [1980] 1 WLR 73, 77). Other examples are *Sargent v Customs and Excise Commissioners* [1994] 1 WLR 235 and *21st Century Logistic Solutions Ltd v Madysen Ltd* [2004] STC 1535, at [19].

Judicial observations that monies subject to a tax claim by HMRC are 'impressed' with that claim, which prevents these monies from being 'possessions' for the purpose of the European Convention of Human Rights (ECHR), Article 1 Protocol 1 (A1P1) (*APVCO 19 Limited and Others v HM Treasury and Another* [2015] STC 2272, at [80] (per Black LJ); *R (Rowe) v HMRC* [2018] STC 462, at [183] (per McCombe LJ)) do not, even on their terms, hold that any sort of 'trust' is imposed on a taxable person's monies and are confined to the construction and application of ECHR A1P1.

A useful (and conclusive) cross-check that tax liabilities are non-proprietary is the absence of any property interest on the part of the tax-creditor on monies transferred to an innocent transferee by a taxable person who has a tax liability. The transferee has no liability at all in respect of the transferor-taxpayer's tax liability to the tax creditor (a tax code may impose a specific deemed liability for tax obligations on particular persons in particular circumstances but the need for such deeming reinforces the soundness of the analysis presented here).

4. FEATURES OF A TAX OBLIGATION SPECIFIC TO ITS BEING A PERSONAL MONETARY OBLIGATION

The personal monetary nature of a tax obligation means that a tax obligation has certain attributes that would not be present in a property obligation.

ECHR A1P1

The case law of the European Court of Human Rights (ECtHR) on retrospective tax legislation assumes the relevant A1P1 possession to be a form of legitimate expectation, a right to be taxed on a non-arbitrary basis and not in the taxable person's monies: *A, B, C and D v United Kingdom (8531/79)* (1981) 23 DR 203 (on whether retrospective taxation was A1P1 compliant); *Voggenberger Transport GmbH v Austria (21294/93)* (1994, unreported); *NAP Holdings UK Limited v United Kingdom (27721/95)* (1996) 22 EHRR CD114 (tax legislation which reflected general practice need not have retrospective effect); *MA v Finland (Admissibility) (27793/95)* (2003) 37 EHRR CD210, followed by the ECtHR in *SB & Others v Finland (30289/96)* (2004, unreported); *Kopecký v Slovakia* (2004) 41 EHRR 944; *NKM v Hungary* [2013] ECHR 430. Philip Baker provides an excellent summary (Baker 2005) of these cases decided by the ECtHR; in particular, *Voggenberger* would not have come to the writer's attention without Baker's summary.

The analysis of the relevant 'possession' in the ECHR jurisprudence is, accordingly, consistent with the analysis of taxation set out in this chapter. However, although the earlier English case law took the same approach (see, for example, *R (Huitson) v HMRC* [2011] STC 1860; *R (ToTel Limited) v First-tier Tribunal Tax Chamber (HM Treasury interested party)* [2011] STC 1485), the Court of Appeal now treats the taxable person's monies as the relevant A1P1 possession: *APVCO 19 Limited and Others v HM Treasury and Another* [2015] STC 2272; *R (Rowe) v HMRC* [2018] STC 462; *Reeves v HMRC* [2018] STC 2056 (TCC). This more recent approach is wrong precisely because taxation does not impose any sort of property obligation.

Which analysis is used makes a real difference. If the correct approach (that is, that the A1P1 possession is a form of legitimate expectation) is taken, the very content of the possession is what the court must grapple with. The question for the court is whether the claim is sufficiently established in the light of the taxing jurisdiction's tax code and case law (including anti-avoidance case law) to amount to an A1P1 'possession'. If it is, the lawfulness of any interference is assessed through the application of the margin of appreciation and proportionality. If, on the other hand, the A1P1 possession is the taxable person's monies, a charge to taxation will automatically interfere with the 'peaceful enjoyment' of property (the monies); the dispute is equally automatically a contest between any margin of appreciation and proportionality. This is a different exercise. Whilst the latter is the approach presently taken in England and Wales, it misidentifies the A1P1 possession by misidentifying the nature of a tax charge.

TAX LIABILITY FOR ILLEGAL ACTS

It is trite law that illegal acts may be taxed: *Mann v Nash* [1932] 1 KB 752; *IRC v Aken* [1990] STC 497. It is perfectly coherent for a legal system simultaneously to sanction an activity which is unlawful and to tax any income from that activity if it satisfies the definition of a 'taxable activity', as long as taxation is properly characterised as a demand enforceable as a non-proprietary debt. The taxing state is not somehow exercising property rights in unlawfully obtained monies. Rather the taxing state is making a demand for an amount of money, computed in respect of a tax base for an activity which happens to be unlawful.

This is the point made in *Mann v Nash*: in seeking to tax the taxpayer on his illegal profits, the Revenue were 'taxing the individual with reference to certain facts. It is not a partner or a sharer in the illegality' (at 759). If the taxing state were to be exercising some sort of a claim over the unlawfully earned monies as such, the taxing state would indeed be 'partners' with the taxable person in an unlawful activity, which would be both incoherent and normatively unattractive.

The acknowledgement that the state may exercise a monetary claim (tax) calculated by reference to profits earned from an unlawful activity in addition to imposing sanctions (monetary or otherwise) as a punishment for that activity is consistent with the state's disapproval of these unlawful acts and avoids any accusation of any 'participation' in that unlawful activity. But this is only possible because of the non-proprietary monetary nature of a tax obligation. A share of unlawful gains, where a person is required to donate a proportion of their gains to the state, is indeed to participate in the unlawful activity. On the other hand, the confiscation of ill-gotten gains as a sanction for breach of a prohibited activity by the state is different to a tax charge (representing an enforcement jurisdiction for the breach of this separate prohibitory rule).

DIRECT TAX-INDIRECT TAX DISTINCTION AND FORMAL AND EFFECTIVE INCIDENCE

The purely monetary nature of a tax charge is a necessary feature of the distinction between 'direct' and 'indirect' taxes, explained in chapter one. It is also necessary to the distinction between the 'formal' and 'effective' incidence of tax. This observation has profound implications for taxation as a juristic concept, since the transfer of the effective incidence of tax to be shifted from the taxpayer to another person is only possible because of the monetary, personal, nature of a tax liability. This point is the foundation of the distinction between 'direct' and 'indirect' taxation.

Quite separately, the prospect of a shift in the effective incidence of taxation shows how a claim for tax on a taxpayer takes its measure (computes the tax base) from activities which have taken place *before* the charge to tax is quantified. Put another way, taxation presupposes activities (governed by their own distinct legal regimes) to have taken place and to have assumed juristic relevance before taxation is applied to those activities. Taxation has nothing to say about the juristic nature or substance of these logically prior activities.

SET OFF

Set off would not be possible for a tax obligation which is a property obligation. But because a tax obligation is a personal (non-proprietary), monetary obligation, a tax obligation may be set off against a cross-claim for a repayment from HMRC. *Mellham Limited v Burton* [2006] UKHL 6 established that such a set off may be successfully deployed to resist a claim for the payment of taxes (even where the claim for repayment only crystallised on a payment of the tax obligation). Thus, taxation shows itself to be within the class of monetary liabilities to which set off, a concept which cannot be coherently applied to property obligations, applies.

A WORD ON WITHHOLDING TAXES

Withholding taxes (taxes imposed on the recipient of monies which statute requires the payer to withhold at source) do not undermine the contention advanced here that a tax obligation is a personal, non-property, monetary obligation. Primary examples in the UK tax code include the PAYE provisions (discussed in chapter one) and the requirement of the payers of certain types of interest (ITA 2007, sections 868, 874) to deduct tax at source.

Deduction of tax at source does not import any proprietary obligation in respect of the tax liability. The payer must withhold a sum of money. The payer has a liability to HMRC (under the UK tax code) to pay that amount. But the payer has the same obligation in relation to that amount as the debtor of any money debt, that is to deliver monetary assets equal to the specified amount (precisely because there is no trust imposed in favour of HMRC in respect of monies withheld to satisfy a tax liability). This is the import of *Attorney-General v Antoine* [1949] 2 All ER 1000. As for the payee, the payer's statutory obligation to withhold tax at source has nothing to say about the juristic nature of the payee's tax liability. If the payer does not withhold tax at source, the payee will not have paid their tax liability (via the withholding mechanism) and the payee will (subject to time limits) be liable to assessment on their receipt. That liability will be satisfied by the delivery of money (however financed) as for any money debt.

MONETARY OBLIGATIONS, AUTONOMY AND PERSONHOOD

Taxation imposed as a monetary liability, rather than a property liability, dilutes the value of the personal attributes of the taxpayer ('personhood'). This is illustrated by the decision of the High Court in *Oram v Johnson* [1980] STC 222. The taxpayer sought to claim as deductible expenditure the value of his labour on improving and enlarging an investment property, valuing his time at £1 an hour. The taxpayer's case failed, on the basis that the notion of deductible 'expenditure', in 'money or money's worth', in what is now TCGA 1992, section 38, which defines allowable expenditure 'excluded the value of personal labour, since his labour did not [diminish] his stock of anything by any precisely ascertainable amount' or '[diminish] the total assets of the person making the expenditure': Penner 2005, 80.

So money and only money is relevant for taxation: the taxable person cannot monetise their personal attributes to affect their tax liability.

It is not normatively attractive to ignore the (relevant) personal attributes of a taxable person altogether in computing a taxable amount. The taxable person in *Oram* had incurred an opportunity cost on any view in devoting his own labour on the investment property (he could have done something else which earned him money). In choosing to do the work himself, rather than to pay someone else to do it, the taxable person gave up his own time and effort, which could be ascribed a value (there was no suggestion that the suggested hourly rate was unreasonable). So the purely monetary nature of a tax obligation is not only made highly visible but unattractively so.

5. IMPLICATIONS FOR OBJECTIVES OF TAXATION

As was observed in chapter one, taxation may seek to fulfil different functions. The personal and monetary nature of a liability to tax has important consequences as to both the efficacy of, and normative considerations applicable to, those different functions.

To the extent that taxation may be funded by monies which are gifted from a person outside the taxing jurisdiction, any citizenship function would be heavily diluted: the burden of a key responsibility would lie with another person, who has no commitment to the jurisdiction. On the other hand, the objectives of the financing of public goods, or the funding of non-public-good governmental activities, are necessarily indifferent to the source of financing.

Taxation imposed to redistribute resources is (insofar as the tax may be funded out of borrowings or gifts), rendered potentially ineffective and may lose normative legitimacy as a result. Any inequality between the nominal taxpayer and the donee of the redistributed resources would remain untouched if a third party, and not the taxpayer, has funded the payment. Similarly, taxation imposed to incentivise or disincentivise particular activities will have no effect at all (and lose legitimacy) if the tax is borne by a person other than the target of the particular incentivising/disincentivising tax charge. The same analysis holds true for taxation imposed as a tool of economic management. A taxpayer may abandon any responsibility to any objective sought by taxation and simply pay their tax.

Finally, lest it be said that these observations are blunted because taxpayers generally pay tax out of their own resources, two responses may be made. First, as a matter of principle, the dilution of responsibility (especially role responsibility) consequent on the monetisation of liabilities is sufficiently analytically important to deserve analysis. Second, the satisfaction of tax obligations by gifts (and the consequent effect on the efficacy of taxation) is not remotely fanciful. Multinational groups of companies will fund companies within a particular tax jurisdiction from equity finance (or indeed favourable loans) as a matter of course, and the finance may well come from outside the taxing jurisdiction. And for individuals, the financing of a UK-resident's tax liability by non-UK resident trustees or family members is an unremarkable circumstance.

The purely monetary personal nature of a tax liability accordingly dilutes notions of responsibility and commitment to the different objectives which taxation may pursue, as well as the effectiveness of the charge to tax itself.

6. A CONTRAST BETWEEN A TAX LIABILITY AND COMPULSORY PURCHASE

Yet another way to expose the distinction between a tax liability and a property obligation is to contrast a tax liability with a compulsory purchase of property. Penner provides a comprehensive contrast between the conceptually (and mutually exclusive) notions of expropriation of property and a money debt claim for taxation. For Penner, expropriation is a forced sale of precisely identified property 'not a claim for any amount of value', because 'that property is what the expropriating authority wants': Penner 2005, 83.

By contrast, taxation is not a 'forced sale'. The state organises critical public functions and supplies services to, or for the benefit of, the population as a whole. It is legitimate to demand payment from persons with a relevant connection to the state to fund those public functions and services. This approach has judicial endorsement: *MacCormick v FCT* (1984) 158 CLR 622, 640. It is easy to agree with Penner that the notion of taxation as a form of compulsory purchase is unintelligible, which provides further confirmation that a tax liability is not any sort of property obligation at all. The converse is also true: compulsory purchase is not a form of tax.

Take a hypothetical provision that demands that all coal companies sell a proportion of their annual coal extracted to a public entity cheap (say at 50 per cent of market value). The public entity might sell that coal at market value and make a profit. The public body might seek to use (and in fact use) the proceeds to finance public goods. So this compulsory purchase has the identical objective of a tax. But this does not make compulsory acquisition a taxation mechanism. (The obligee may of course have a claim under A1P1 in relation to this compulsory purchase; its status as a 'non-tax' is irrelevant.)

It may be different if the acquisition (at a low price) was followed by a compulsory sale back (at market value) to the coal producer itself, since there is no acquisition and resale of coal in truth at all. The sale and resale are both illusory and what occurs is an extraction of cash from the coal producer (whereas a true compulsory acquisition extracts property, here coal). The loss of potential profit is a not 'tax' (the taxable amount is generally computed on profits, once computed, where profits comprise the tax base: see chapter one).

That the objectives of distinct legal or commercial mechanisms might be the same does not mean that they become legal or commercial mechanisms with the same juristic nature. This is simply modalism in action. Tax law itself recognises this. A company might be financed by preference shares which yield dividends rather than by way of loan which yield interest: the tax code treats dividends and interest as quite separate taxable items (ITTOIA 2005, Part 4, Chapter 2 which relates to the taxation of interest and Chapter 3 and Chapter 4 which deal with the taxation of dividends). In general, (non-tax) law, a contract which yields an annuity and an interest possession trust which yields a regular source of income to the life tenant may give rise to identical amounts of monies to the identical recipient for identical reasons (to finance the recipient) but the contract is not a trust.

The second key idea about tax (that tax is a personal, non-proprietary money obligation) establishes the nature of a tax obligation and its juristic consequences. This foundation allows us to proceed to define 'tax law' as a distinct area of law and to distinguish other money debts from a 'tax', which is the burden of chapter four.

A final word about tithes. If a 'tithe' is an obligation to deliver a proportion of particular property (say corn), then this is a compulsory acquisition of that property. It is not a 'tax' any more than the coal described above (and any debate as to whether it ought to be called a 'tax' becomes a quibble about definitions). If the obligee is entitled to deliver an amount of corn equivalent to the required proportion of their own corn, then the obligation behaves more like money (it is non-proprietorial, albeit that the obligation is in money's worth, not money). Then, depending on whether this obligation arises because of connecting factors and whether there is a putative taxable activity, such an obligation may well be a 'tax'.

RESPONSE TO CHAPTER THREE

RT HON JAMES WOLFFE KC FRSE; DEAN OF THE FACULTY OF ADVOCATES 2014–16; LORD ADVOCATE 2016–21; JUDGE OF APPEAL IN GUERNSEY AND JERSEY

The key message of this chapter is that, at least in the UK tax system, a tax liability is of the nature of a personal debt with HMRC the creditor and the taxpayer the debtor. HMRC has no proprietary right in any specific asset of the taxpayer. If this may seem obvious, it is, as the author effectively demonstrates, well worth stating. He shows that this foundational feature of the UK tax system has analytical, practical and normative consequences. In chapter six, he illustrates how discussion by political philosophers about taxation proceeds without attending to the juristic nature of a tax liability and is the poorer as a result.

The author is surely correct to insist on the importance of analytical accuracy. But although HMRC does not have proprietary rights in any specific asset, a tax liability does – like other debts – diminish the taxpayer's patrimony assessed on a balance sheet basis, and this may have legal and normative consequences. In the context of A1P1, Lord Reed has observed (*Axa v Lord Advocate* [2012] 1 AC 868, at [114]):

> The concept of 'possessions' has been interpreted by [the Strasbourg] Court as including a wide range of economic interests and assets, but one paradigm example of a possession is a person's financial resources. … In the case of an insurance company, the fund out of which it meets claims must therefore constitute a possession within the meaning of the Article. Legislation which has the object and effect of establishing a new category of claims, and which in consequence diminishes the fund, can accordingly be regarded as an interference with that possession.

Further, although HMRC's rights against the taxpayer creditor are personal, this does not mean that tax debts are just the same as other debts. The mechanisms for crystallising a tax liability are different. In Scotland, HMRC may use summary warrant procedure to obtain authority to attach specific assets. And in insolvency (where the distinction between personal and real rights is most sharply at issue) HMRC has the benefit of Crown preference.

Thus, although a tax liability is not, as the author shows, an expropriation of (specific) property, it diminishes the taxpayer's patrimony. And although tax is as the author points out, indifferent as to whether taxpayers pay the liability themselves or through the beneficence of generous relatives, it does entitle the tax authority, ultimately, to use legal process to secure payment from the taxpayer's own assets (if any). It is accordingly of the nature of a tax that it ultimately entitles a public authority to take a taxpayer's resources and to apply them to public purposes. The large questions of political philosophy, as to when and how this is justified, are not answered here – and, as the author argues, should be sensitive to the different purposes which tax may pursue. But that is not the author's purpose and he is surely right to insist that political philosophers who debate these issues should do so on sound premises. His novel and important work, through fundamental analysis, discloses what those premises are.

Author's response: Mr Wolffe is right (on any view) that a personal monetary obligation impacts upon a debtor's patrimony, as a notional liability on a notional balance sheet. And the (obiter) observations of Lord Reed in Axa *about the Strasbourg case law are consistent with the ratio of post-*Huitson *English authority. But of course, as observed in this chapter, this approach automatically engages A1P1 in every case a tax charge is imposed and sets up the contest between the margin of appreciation and proportionality, whereas the Strasbourg case law is both consistent with the personal nature of a tax obligation and addresses properly the prior question of whether there is an A1P1 possession at all, which is why this chapter questions the recent English approach. As for the ability of a creditor ultimately to enforce a personal debt ultimately against the debtor's assets, these contingent rights do not affect the personal nature of the original obligation. And they attract different questions of both principle and policy as to their legitimacy to those which arise in relation to the original debt. So a tax obligation necessitates two conversations about legitimacy: one about the original tax debt and another about its enforcement.*

4

'Tax Law' is a Distinct Area of Law

1. INTRODUCTION

Chapters one, two and three give a picture of what a tax charge looks like from the perspective of the jurist. We can now apply the analyses set out in those chapters to compare and contrast a tax obligation with other monetary obligations and to demonstrate that a tax obligation can always be identified as distinct from these other money obligations. This secures tax law's status as a distinct and coherent area of law, capable of precise definition.

The key idea is that tax law is distinct from other areas of law, and that its distinct juristic identity needs to be articulated with precision – not just for legal philosophers but because of the practical effect which this exercise has for the interpretation and application of critical statutory provisions.

Consider sub-sections 14(2) and (3) of the Retained EU Law (Revocation and Reform) Act 2023. This provides that a Minister (or a devolved legislature) may repeal secondary retained EU Law, with the option of replacing it with regulations of the same, or similar or alternative objectives as they consider 'appropriate'. In doing so, the Minister (or devolved legislature) may, under section 14(4), enact regulations which:

> may create a criminal offence that corresponds or is similar to a criminal offence created by secondary retained EU law revoked by the regulations ... may provide for the imposition of monetary penalties in cases that correspond or are similar to cases in which secondary retained EU law revoked by the regulations enables monetary penalties to be imposed ... may provide for the charging of fees [but] ... (f) *may not – (i) impose taxation* ... (emphasis added)

This extraordinarily wide Henry VIII power (being a power of the executive to amend or repeal primary Acts of Parliament) has one critical limitation: that a Minister may not 'impose taxation'. Thus, the difference between a criminal fine or a monetary penalty and a tax is critical. That the 'tax' caveat is an application of the prohibition in the Bill of Rights and the Claim of Right that the executive cannot impose a tax charge does not take one very far. One cannot run away from the task of identifying whether a particular imposition falls on one side of this line or the other by observing that 'tax' may mean different things in different contexts, so there is somehow no need to undertake this task. 'Tax' is nowhere defined in the 2023 Act. As it happens, in both the UK and non-UK case law examined below, 'tax' (where this notion is central to the case) is not said (in any of these cases) to take a specific meaning peculiar to its statutory or constitutional context (for example, in the United States Constitution). So it is not a sterile exercise in essentialism to identify a core meaning of the term 'tax'. It is an exercise which the legislature (and other legislatures around the world) require us to not just to undertake but to complete. The answer will, in the case of section 14 of the 2023 Act, have important work to do in defining the limits of this wide delegated power.

The definition of 'tax' is found in the model of a tax charge discussed in chapter one. This model is central to the identification of 'tax' as a distinct area of law and chapter one should be read in conjunction with this chapter. To revisit the conclusions of chapter one, a 'tax' charge is a charge to a monetary obligation which is predicated on (1) a person undertaking a putative taxable activity and (2) that person (or that activity) having sufficient attributes which 'connect' them to the taxing jurisdiction (for our purposes, tax residence or source) and (3) a 'taxable amount' being computed in respect of the taxable activity. Any obligation (monetary or otherwise) which arises by reason of a person satisfying different conditions is not a 'tax' as a matter of law.

A common feature of the various definitions of taxation which have been advanced from time to time, whether by economists, in existing literature or in case law, is the absence of any analytical foundation. We will consider some current definitions of taxation and point out why these are, for one reason or another, deficient and then revisit section 14 of the 2023 Act in the light of the model discussed in chapter one to provide an intelligible, predictable and consistent approach which gives 'tax' a distinct and coherent meaning for this and other statutory purposes.

2. ACCOUNTING, TREASURY AND ECONOMISTS' DEFINITIONS

Definitions provided by accounting and treasury bodies rely on references to 'government' purposes and to the notion that taxation is 'compulsory'. They further expressly distinguish taxation from other liabilities, such as a liability to pay for goods or services and criminal fines. These approaches lead to an over-inclusive definition of taxation.

The Organisation for Economic Co-operation and Development (OECD) defines taxes as 'compulsory unrequited payments to general government or to a supranational authority': OECD 2021, A.2.1. 'Unrequited' in this context means that the payer does not receive benefits proportionate to the payments. The OECD draws a distinction between taxation and: (1) fines and penalties, including tax-related fines and penalties (A.2.2 and A.2.20; SNA 1993, paragraphs 2.12–2.24) and (2) 'user fees' paid for services or activities. However, if such fees greatly exceed the cost of provision or the fees are payable by a person who does not benefit from them, or where there is no identifiable benefit in return for the payment (for example, a payment for a fishing licence where the licence does not confer specific fishing rights), or where any benefit is not proportionate to the payments made by each payer, the OECD considers the fees to be 'taxes'.

Similarly, HM Treasury's Classification Paper defines taxes by reference to international guidelines as 'compulsory, unrequited payments in cash or in kind which are levied by general government, or by the Institutions of the European Union': (HM Treasury 2013, 2.4; by reference to the European System of Accounts (European Commission 2010) 4.14. A similar definition is used in the System of National Accounts (IMF 2008) section C, paragraph 8.52.

Economists' definitions are similar. For example, Hyman states by way of a definition of taxes that 'the principal means of financing government expenditures, are compulsory payments that do not necessarily bear any direct relationship to the benefits of government goods and services received': Hyman 1990, 23. 'Compulsory' is understood as denoting a situation in which there is 'no reasonable alternative' to making the payment. To this is added the idea that payments of tax are 'unrequited', in an attempt to distinguish taxation from user charges and to exclude from the definition of 'tax' a payment for goods and services in competitive marketplaces: OECD 2021, 2.5, 2.6.

All of these very similar definitions of taxation are simultaneously over-restrictive and over-expansive.

To take the first of the attributes said to be a feature of 'taxation', taxes need not, in fact, be paid to 'general government'. While of course almost all taxes (and all taxes in the UK tax code) are payable to public bodies, the English Court of Appeal has expressly acknowledged the prospect that taxes may be payable to non-governmental bodies: *Aston Cantlow and Wilmcote with Billesley Church Council v Wallbank* [2002] STC 313 (EWCA) ('*Aston Cantlow (CA)*'); overruled on other grounds in the House of Lords *Parochial Church Council of the Parish of Aston Cantlow and Wilmcote with Billesley v Wallbank* [2003] UKHL 37 ('*Aston Cantlow (HL)*') and therefore still authority on this point. Australian case law takes the same approach (see below). Thus, the payment of monies to government (or to 'supra-government') is not a necessary feature of a tax: to make this part of the definition is too restrictive.

The fact that taxes need not be paid to government is in fact tacitly acknowledged by the OECD, which includes church taxes if the church is 'part of central government' and payments to 'fiscal monopolies [not restricted to any central government role, so, for example, nationalised utilities which are monopolistic] ... which reflect the exercise of ... taxing power': A.2.6, which shows that the notion of payments to 'government' is too restrictive. A church's role in central government may be ceremonial only and be hedged with conventions about the relationship between church and state, at least in most contemporary states. So the extension of 'taxation' to church taxes is a material qualification to the OECD's initial definition of 'taxation'. And, as observed, a fiscal monopoly need play no part in government at all for its profits to be considered 'taxes', which is a greater qualification still.

The term 'compulsory' in the various definitions referred to above merely excludes voluntary payments and restricts taxation to payments made to satisfy a legal obligation. But many legal obligations (for example, contractual obligations) have nothing to do with taxation. Equally, any extension of 'taxation' to encompass 'economic compulsion' – for example, a nominally voluntary payment, absent which the payer could not function (say a weekly 'voluntary' donation by a shop owner to a political party, absent which the shop owner would have to close down) would clothe commercial extortion (whether lawful or not) with the status of 'tax'. This would not be juristically helpful. It does not help to

identify the specific attributes of a lawful tax; it also obscures any normative assessment of the payment obligation: what should be scrutinised
is the justification for compelling the shop owner to make the payment
to the political party, not whether this payment is part of the payer's 'tax
base'.

The idea that the payment is 'unrequited' is no more helpful. This
attribute merely presages the express distinction between taxation and
'user fees'. This negative definition of tax (tax is not a user fee) does not
tell us what tax *is*. The same is true for the distinction between taxation
and fines and penalties.

Furthermore, the express extension of 'taxation' to the monies paid
as consideration for services (or other 'activities') where there is no
(identifiable) benefit to the payer, or an absence of any proportionate
connection between payment and benefit, is over-expansive. An over-
charge for services is exactly that. To be sure, the overcharge may well
'be' – in the sense of represent for payer or payee – a charge 'for' the
services even if it is the fruit of commercial extortion. But it is a non-
sequitur to term the overcharge a 'tax'.

It is true that courts must grapple with charges which, although
in form a permitted charge for services, are, in fact, a (prohibited)
disguised customs duty. In such cases, the disguise is stripped away by
considering the purpose of the charge and its commercial relationship
to what it is purportedly being charged for: for the purposes of the
Treaty for the Functioning of the European Union, Article 28: *EC v Italy*
('Italian Art') Case 7/68; *Bresciani* Case 87/75. But the possibility of
legal relativism (where something is legally 'X' for one legal purpose but
not 'X' for another legal purpose) is well-established. So 'shares' empty
of any economic interest in the issuing company are, indeed, 'shares'
for company law purposes but are not for the purposes of creating a
tax-privileged group where economic substance matters: *Collector of
Stamp Revenue v Arrowtown Assets Ltd* [2003] HKCFA 46. Nevertheless,
the utility (and need) to identify the core meaning of legal concepts,
including 'tax', remains.

Of course, courts should leave room for any term, including 'tax',
to be given a special extended or restricted meaning appropriate to any
particular legislative context. But there will be occasions where a term has
a default meaning which, if nothing else, should serve as a starting point,
and this default meaning should be neither over-expansive nor unduly
restrictive, whilst seeking to accommodate the necessary attributes which
must be present to fall within the ambit of the term in question.

A further complaint about the definitions of taxation considered above is the failure to acknowledge the modal nature of taxation. There is no acknowledgement of the diverse functions which taxation may seek to achieve. The variety of functions which taxation may seek to achieve necessarily informs taxation's juristic nature and any definition must therefore accommodate this modality. By focusing on the juristic anatomy of taxation, the definition given in chapter one accomplishes this.

3. JUDICIAL DEFINITIONS

The definitions of taxation discussed above were not legal definitions, so it might be unfair to criticise these as they did not purport to offer the answer to legal questions posed by provisions such as section 14 of the 2023 Act. The authors of these definitions had a different agenda: scrutinising executive action (analysing public finance generally and the efficiency of fiscal measure specifically). But they comprise important material, since they inevitably will be a port of call (even if not the first) for a court seeking to answer a question as to what is a 'tax'. And they are unsatisfactory.

However, when we turn to judicial definitions of a charge to 'tax', we find that these formulations (all advanced in Commonwealth jurisdictions; with perhaps one exception, the UK case law is spectacularly unhelpful) are no more useful than the treasury or economic definitions discussed above. They have traditionally defined tax as a charge which is '(1) enforceable by law; (2) imposed under the authority of the legislature; (3) levied by a public body; and (4) intended for a public purpose': *Lawson v Interior Tree Fruit and Vegetable Committee of Direction* [1931] SCR 357, 363 (per Duff J).

Although these observations were obiter, the levies in question being held to be ultra vires the charging authority because of the restrictions they presented to interprovincial trade (irrespective of their status as 'taxes'), this formulation was central to the decision in *Re Eurig* (1998) 165 DLR (4th) 1, 10. In *Re Eurig* the status of probate fees as 'taxes' (on the *Lawson* formulation: see paragraph [15] at 576) meant that they were ultra vires because all 'taxes' had to originate in the legislature and these particular fees had been unlawfully levied instead by the Canadian Governor in Council.

This formulation has been consistently taken up in specialist text-books on UK tax law (see for example Lee et al 2016, 4; Smith 2015, 4). For a brief descriptive comparative treatment on the meaning of 'tax' (albeit with no analysis of the juristic or normative merits of particular meanings) see Thuronyi, Brooks and Kolozs 2016, 39–46. It is different from the definitions discussed above but is also unsatisfactory in principle. It has not been analysed or defended on any principled basis, either in *Lawson* or *Re Eurig*, or in any subsequent judgment. They are simply taken as given (see *Lawson* at 363; *Re Eurig* at [15] simply cites *Lawson* without any analysis). It is convenient to take in turn each feature ascribed to taxation by this formulation.

ENFORCEABLE BY LAW

This feature simply recognises that taxation must be lawful: that taxation must meet the membership criteria (the terminology is that of Raz 1980, 1–2) of the legal system which claims to impose a charge to tax. It follows that a claim for taxation 'can [lawfully] be sued for': *Lawson* at 363 per Duff J. There is nothing particular to taxation, as opposed to any other branch of law (for example, the enforcement of a contractual debt) about this characteristic. And it is unhelpful to go to any great length to distinguish taxation from voluntary payments on the one hand or monies payable not by reason of legal obligation but under economic compulsion on the other, for the reasons given.

COMPULSORY

Compulsion is a feature often appealed to both in judicial and institutional definitions. An example is Lord Sumner's statement in *City of Halifax v Nova Scotia Car Works Ltd* [1914] AC 992, at 998: '[T]he essence of taxation is that it is imposed by superior authority without the taxpayer's consent, except in so far as representative government operates by the consent of the taxpayer.' If this simply means that a 'tax' is imposed as an exercise of prescriptive jurisdiction, it is unexceptionable. However, the notion of compulsion has been characterised as being 'a practical compulsion', or a 'practical and legal necessity': *Re Eurig*, at [15].

A 'broad' version of compulsion is deployed by Bowler Smith and Ostik to classify the Central London Congestion Charge as a 'tax': Bowler Smith and Ostik 2011, 492, appealing to the HM Treasury Classification Paper 'Class (2010) 2 Receipts', March 2010, PU975b. There is no explanation or analysis as to what is meant by 'broad', or the limits (if any) to be applied to the notion of 'compulsion'. The absence of a 'reasonable alternative' to payment of the liability is a necessary condition for taxation. But what does this mean? If it is a synonym for the sort of commercial extortion of a payment for a supposedly voluntary activity referred to above (the donation to a political party required to keep a shop open), this simply treats extortion as a form of taxation, and, as discussed above, this is not a useful extension of the concept of taxation. But if the notion of compulsion relates to an avoidable activity (in the sense that a person need not do that activity and thus avoid the 'compulsory' payment), the payment is not 'compulsory' at all, as the payment may be avoided simply by not carrying out the activity which gives rise to the payment. (Bowler Smith and Ostik themselves seem to accept this at 494.)

This is not, of course, to say that taxes must be avoidable by desisting from undertaking taxable activities; it may be that certain taxes are not avoidable. But the point made here is that some obligations which are taxes on any view may be avoided by not undertaking taxable activities which makes the Bowler Smith and Ostik notion of 'compulsion' unworkable. If the notion of 'compulsion' is extended to notions of 'practical' compulsion and not restricted to an exercise of prescriptive jurisdiction, it becomes incoherent.

Bowler Smith and Ostik cite two cases in support of their broad conception of taxation. The first, *Attorney-General (New South Wales) v Homebush Flour Mills Ltd* [1936] 56 CLR 390 is irrelevant to the juristic definition of taxation, as the court relied on the concept of 'compulsion' not to distinguish 'compulsory' taxes from 'voluntary' user fees, but to reveal the true nature of an illusory 'option' in a scheme. The second case, *Bolt v City of Lansing* 587 N.W. 2d 264 (Mich 1998) (discussed in Bowler Smith and Ostik, at 492), distinguishes between 'compulsory' taxation in respect of activities which could realistically not be done at all and voluntary user charges. It therefore assumes that 'tax' on activities which may voluntarily be undertaken or not is 'compulsory', which is, for the reasons given above, confused. Thus, neither case shores up the notion of 'compulsion' to which Bowler Smith and Ostik appeal.

'Compulsion', as a feature of taxation, is therefore either incoherent or redundant, insofar as it is extended to anything beyond an exercise of prescriptive jurisdiction. In either case, this attribute should be jettisoned as a necessary feature of taxation.

LEGISLATIVE SOURCE

So far as the UK tax code is concerned, all of the taxes imposed by primary Acts of Parliament represent an exercise of Parliament's unlimited continuing sovereignty: Goldsworthy 1999; Elliott and Thomas 2014, 212 et seq. The power to tax is generally viewed as a hallmark of legislative sovereignty. In *Brown (Surveyor of Taxes) v National Provident Institution* [1921] 2 AC 222, 257 Lord Sumner said: 'It is a most wholesome rule that in taxing the subject the Crown must show that clear powers to tax were given by the Legislature.' Only Parliament may impose taxation; the executive has no inherent power to impose tax through the prerogative (Bill of Rights 1689, Article 4 in England, and Claim of Right 1689 in Scotland; *Congreve v Home Office* [1976] QB 629) but only has 'collection and management' powers to administer the tax code as enacted by Parliament (TMA 1970, section 1).

It is true that the Bill of Rights, which prohibits the levying of monetary impositions without clear legislative authority, supports a constrained approach to ascertaining whether there is a power to tax. So, in the absence of legislation, the Crown cannot charge licence fees relating to the distribution of milk: *Attorney-General v Wilts United Dairies* [1921] 37 TLR 884, 885 (per Bankes LJ), 885–86 per Scrutton LJ), and 886 (per Atkin LJ); nor may the Crown collect income tax not yet imposed by an Act of Parliament, albeit already approved by a resolution of the Committee of the House of Commons: *Bowles v Bank of England* [1913] 1 Ch 57, 84 (per Parker J).

But a tax charge could arise at common law (ie have a non-statutory source), without any infringement of the Bill of Rights by the executive. A taxable person, a tax base, a tax rate and tax compliance and enforcement measures may all be a function of common law. While a common law tax charge is inevitably vulnerable to a charge (at least) of being undemocratic, the source of the liability need not (and in the case of taxation does not) dictate its juristic nature a priori.

The charge scrutinised by the Court of Appeal in *Aston Cantlow* (CA) arose at common law and at no stage did the Court of Appeal suggest that a non-legislative source of itself deprived an obligation to pay monies of its character as a 'tax' obligation, if the obligation was otherwise properly so characterised (the decision was overruled on other grounds in the House of Lords and is still binding authority on this point). The Court of Appeal's decision is discussed in greater detail below. Thus the 'legislative source' condition for taxation is wrong, both in principle and as a matter of English authority.

PUBLIC BODY

At least one commentator has developed the notion that taxation is necessarily imposed by a public body in the context of 'defining the reciprocal duties of State and individuals': Snape 2011, at 36 (citing Allen 1995, 300 and Loughlin 2010, 446). Taxation is, on this view, an instance of constitutional and administrative law. Taxation serves to advance the 'public interest', establish and regulate government authority and maintain state authority (albeit constrained by constitutional principles): Snape 2011, at 168–69. But the proposition that taxation is necessarily imposed by a public body is mistaken. Furthermore, the proposition that taxation must be imposed by a public body bleeds into the proposition that taxation must serve a 'public' purpose, which is also wrong: see below.

The notion that a tax is necessarily imposed by a 'public' body has been rejected in terms by Australian case law (as has the proposition that taxation must serve a 'public purpose'). See *Australian Tape Manufacturers Association v Commonwealth* (1993) 176 CLR 480, at 501 (per Mason CJ, delivering the judgment of the majority):

> It is scarcely to be contemplated that the character of an impost as a tax depends upon whether the authority is a public authority … it is not essential to the concept of a tax that the exaction should be done by a public authority.

To be sure, virtually all tax liabilities are statutory and are imposed by public bodies, such as central or local government; but as *Aston Cantlow* (CA) makes clear, this is not a necessary condition for a liability to pay monies to be a 'tax' liability. While it is easy to agree that, to the extent that taxation is imposed by a sovereign public body, taxation may be an expression of sovereignty and that any public body which imposes taxation is subject to the constitutional and administrative law constraints which apply to that particular tax-imposing public body, these propositions do not entail that non-public bodies cannot impose 'taxation' as a matter of general jurisprudential principle (or even as a matter of legality in the UK).

PUBLIC PURPOSES

That tax must be imposed for a 'public purpose' has been described as 'a core element of identifying a charge as a tax in modern taxation': Bhandari 2017, 2. The 'public purpose' rationale is assumed to be a necessary component of taxation in the extant literature which reaches for a juristic definition of taxation: see, for example, Barassi 2005, 73. These commentators provide no analytical basis for this proposition in their definitions of taxation, which reduces the notion of 'public purpose' as a necessary component of taxation to a mere assertion without foundation.

A 'public purpose' condition for a liability to be a tax liability is also present in some Commonwealth case law, although again there is no analytical defence of this approach: *Fairfax v Federal Commissioner of Taxation* (1965) 114 CLR 1, 19 (per Windeyer J). 'Public purpose', as a contradistinction from consideration for goods or services, has been advanced as a feature of taxation, again without analytical foundation: *Airservices Australia v Canadian Airlines International Limited* (1999) 202 CLR 133, [132] (per Gaudron J), citing Latham CJ in *Matthews v Chicory Marketing Board* (Vict) (1983) 60 CLR 263, 276. The reference to taxation *not* being a payment for services, replicated in definitions of taxation provided by treasury and accounting bodies, does not help to tell us what tax *is*, as discussed above.

As it happens, the public purpose condition has been firmly rejected in Australia in *Air Caledonie International v Commonwealth* (1988) 165 CLR 462, 467 (cited with approval by the majority in *Australian Tape Manufacturers Association*, 504). This decision is correct in principle, even though it is not informed by any more analysis than the contrary principles discussed in the previous paragraph.

In fact, the 'public purpose' requirement is redundant at best and misleading at worst. If a public purpose is simply a synonym for the purposes to which a public body which lawfully raises tax may apply or chooses to apply tax revenues (or, indeed, the purposes for which the public body levies the tax), this notion adds nothing to the (misconceived) proposition that taxation must be raised by a public body. If the notion of a 'public purpose' seeks to add a further juristic criterion for taxation, this approach is also misconceived. Suppose that a 'public' purpose is a purpose which, in contradistinction to a 'private' or 'personal' purpose, has as its object an effect or consequence upon some or all of the populace within a particular jurisdiction. The modal nature of taxation soon unravels the suggestion that taxation must be underpinned by a public purpose.

For example, the finance of non-public goods or services is not a public service, since the taxing state is simply financing the provision of goods or services which the public may choose to consume or not, perhaps in competition with private competitors. Taxation here is financing a body (albeit a 'public' body) in its capacity as a private operator. Indeed, all tax receipts may be spent by the taxing authority for any purpose within its vires, which may or may not be a 'public' purpose, for instance financing beneficiaries of the Civil List, furnishing the dwelling place of the Lord Chancellor with expensive wallpaper, or paying the salaries of a private company which benefits from a bail-out. It is not obvious that there is a 'public' *purpose* to such expenditure, especially if the beneficiaries do not carry out any public functions.

So far as taxation imposed by the legislature within the UK is concerned, any juristic definition which seeks to confine taxation to monies raised for 'public' purposes (assuming the charge to be lawful) conflicts with Parliamentary sovereignty. Parliament can raise funds through taxation for whatever ends it likes. Nor is any such restriction justified by conventional notions of tax jurisdiction in public international law.

CONCLUSION ON DEFINITIONS OF TAXATION

None of the definitions of taxation considered in this chapter are supported by any analysis. To aggregate the features attributed to taxation in these definitions, taxation must (1) be enforceable by law, (2) be 'compulsory' (in a way distinct from being 'enforceable by law'), (3) have a legislative source, (4) be raised by a 'public' body, (5) be raised for a 'public' or 'governmental' purpose and (6) be 'unrequited'. While one or all these purported attributes of taxation may be found in a particular tax, none of them are either necessary or sufficient juristic features of a definition of taxation. These features are considered above individually. Adding them together does not help. The definitions remain at the same time too wide and too restrictive, remaining entirely unhelpful in the jurisprudential analysis undertaken here. Orthodox definitions of taxation are therefore inadequate, with the result that analyses reliant on such definitions are faulty.

4. TAXATION INDIVIDUATED

'Individuation', to adapt the terminology of Professor Joseph Raz (Raz 1980, especially Chapters III–V), is the organisation of legal material to form distinct, coherent bodies of law. The model described in chapter one individuates taxation as that area of law where an obligation arises by reason of the application of the provisions which identify a taxable person, which in turn require the identification of a tax base, the setting of a tax rate and the imposition of tax compliance and enforcement obligations. The specific content of the connecting factors (generally residence and source) which convert the putative taxable activity into a taxable activity and the person undertaking that activity into a taxable person (recollecting the modal and personal, monetary nature of a tax obligation as discussed in chapter two and chapter three), is what individuates taxation and distinguishes taxation from other money obligations (even those with the same objectives as a particular tax).

This individuated formulation, captured in the model of a tax charge in chapter one (and the foundational status of the rules which define a taxable person) accommodates the personal, monetary nature of a tax obligation and taxation's modal nature. Indeed, taxation has been described in almost precisely these terms, both judicially (*Pryce & Ors v Monmouthshire Canal and Railway Companies* (1879) 4 App Cas 197, 202–03 (per Lord Cairns LC)) and in discussions of the historical relationship between taxation and markets (Innes 1913, 398, cited in Fox and Ernst 2016, 639), although not sufficiently often so as to make this individuated description of a tax liability orthodoxy.

We now turn to see (1) how this individuation exercise differentiates taxation from other money obligations, and (2) that this individuated conception of tax law is consistent with authority. These exercises allow us to revisit section 14 of the 2023 Act and apply the chapter one model of a tax charge to distinguish between the imposition of an impermissible tax and the imposition of permitted penalties or fines.

HOW TO DISTINGUISH TAX FROM OTHER MONEY OBLIGATIONS

There are of course different types of money obligation. Other than a tax obligation, a money debt may also arise, most commonly: (1) as consideration payable for the delivery of goods or services (which include 'user charges'); (2) as a liability to pay a civil penalty; (3) as a liability to pay a criminal fine; and (4) as a liability to pay damages in tort. A tax obligation is distinct in legal nature from all of these other money obligations. The application of the chapter one model to identify what separates a tax obligation from each of these other money obligations, even where a tax obligation and a money obligation seek to achieve the same objective, not only exposes that the legal rules which impose different money obligations are identifiably different but also reveals that despite having similar objectives, these different rules (and the different money obligations they give rise to) represent different types of legal norm.

TAX DISTINGUISHED FROM CONSIDERATION FOR SERVICES ('USER CHARGES')

The liability to pay consideration for services reflects a legal norm that once services have been supplied the recipient incurs a liability to pay for them – generally as a matter of agreement between the parties but sometimes on other principles of the law of obligations. Put another way, there is no exercise of prescriptive jurisdiction or other common law unilateral imposition of an obligation to pay. Liability to pay consideration is very far from the connecting factors which legitimise the imposition of a monetary obligation to pay a taxing authority because a person undertakes a putative taxable activity which requires the computation of positive and negative amounts to yield a net taxable amount. The legitimisation of those connecting factors is informed by different legal norms to those which enforce a bargain or otherwise arise within the law of obligations.

So it is easy to identify and distinguish an obligation to pay consideration for services from a tax charge which arises from the undertaking of a putative taxable activity by a person who is sufficiently connected to the taxing jurisdiction through tax residence or source. There is no need to incorporate a definitional distinction between the two for these distinct obligations to be readily identified as distinct legal concepts. The same analysis can be applied to the provision of goods.

But what of excessive amounts charged by (say) a public body for services? Might such an excessive charge be a disguised 'tax' and, if so, ought not such a feature be built into the definition of 'tax' (to include excessive consideration and to exclude a 'proper' consideration)? The short answers are 'yes' but only on special occasions, otherwise 'no'.

The EU case law (*EC v Italy* ('Italian Art') and *Bresciani* discussed above) on disguised customs duties assumes that an over-charge for services at the border of an EU Member State is indeed a prohibited 'tax'. This assumption is a necessary implication of the internal market regime. In a legal world in which if one EU Member State imposed its own customs duties this would fatally undermine the common EU system of tariffs, it is unsurprising that a charge which is levied for the 'general interest', the quantum of which is a function of the quantity of goods entering a particular Member State, is assumed to be a disguised customs duty (a tax). But this special legislative assumption does not, on any view, hold good for all provisions which need an answer to what is a 'tax'. And as also observed above, there is no reason to suppose that 'tax' (like most legal terms) does not have an intelligible, orthodox meaning, albeit that it may be subject to modification in particular contexts.

However, the search for some precise distinction between user charges and tax charges as a method of defining taxation generically is deep-rooted in the existing literature and some Commonwealth case law: see Bowler Smith and Ostik 2011 for extensive examples. A paradigm example is *Re Eurig Estate*, in which the Canadian Supreme Court held that an *ad valorem* probate fee was a tax rather than a fee for services, because of 'the absence of a nexus between the levy and the cost of the service'. The Canadian Supreme Court therefore suggested that where there is no commercial connection ('nexus') between services and payments, the payments cannot be payments for services and must be a tax. This reasoning is an example of the mistaken assumption that a service provider can only provide an over-priced service by imposing a 'tax' on the excessive element of the price.

Ironically, tax and user fees have, on occasion, been treated judicially as identical: the Australian High Court in *Air Caledonie* has said that

> [in] one sense, all taxes exacted by a national government and paid into national revenue can be described as 'fees for services'. They are fees which the resident or visitor is required to pay as the quid pro quo for the totality of benefits and services which he receives from governmental sources.

This conflation of 'tax' and 'user fees' is wrong in principle. Taxation to raise revenue to pay for public goods cannot be aptly described as a payment for 'services', certainly not by those who do not receive particular benefits for which tax revenues pay. A state is not, on any view, a mere provider of services and public functions cannot be described as such. A closer analogy is a compulsory contribution to a common fund, where the contributor may or may not be within the class of beneficiaries (or even if they are, may never benefit from the fund). But even this analogy fails, since it fails to accommodate the other functions which taxation may seek to fulfil (redistribution, (dis)incentivisation of particular activities, economic tools and the funding of governmental commercial activities) and which cannot reasonably be described as 'services' at all. So not only is the conflation of tax with some sort of 'fee' inapt, but on no view is this approach in *Air Caledonie* a complete definition of 'tax'.

To define tax by reference to user charges (by exclusion or inclusion) does not work. As observed above, there is simply no basis to treat every over-charge for goods or services as a 'tax'. This is true even if a 'tax' might somehow be described as a payment for services. A public body may over-charge simply as an exercise of raw commercial power, in the same manner as a private commercial operator. There is even less reason to treat a 'tax' as being a 'user charge' for services, when it may be imposed to serve a variety of purposes and where not all of the public functions which it may fund can reasonably be characterised as a 'service'.

So observations that taxes 'do not necessarily bear any direct relationship to the benefits of government goods and services received' (see Hyman 1990 above), or that '[a] charge [can be] out of all proportion with the service being provided' (OECD 2021 at A.2), whilst true, are irrelevant to a generic definition of 'tax' (see also Bowler Smith and Ostik 2011, 488, who advance a test of a payment yielding a 'significant profit level' where there is 'evidence, but uncertainty or disagreement as to the level of service provision to the payer' to determine that payment to be a 'tax').

Indeed, any attempt to define tax by reference to a relationship between the charge and the costs of production involves an extremely imprecise and difficult exercise. To scrutinise the relationship between costs of supply and charges, in order to identify a charge as a 'tax' charge or consideration for those goods or services raises many questions, not least whether the notion of an 'excessive' cost is subjective or objective, whether there is a threshold over which any charge ceases to be a charge for goods or services and becomes a 'tax', and which 'costs' of the supplier are to be taken in to account in any evaluation of whether the charge for goods or services is 'excessive'. These difficulties are not addressed in any of the literature which advocates a link between the level of a charge and services provided: see for example Bowler Smith and Ostik 2011 at 488, who merely postulate a 'tax' to be a fee which is for services but at a level which is 'over and above an appropriate or reasonable market rate of return'. On the other hand, a juristic definition of taxation which relies on the components discussed in chapter one – identifying a taxable person as one who undertakes a taxable activity and who has a sufficient connecting factor – automatically and adequately excludes consideration for goods or services from the definition of 'tax'.

This analysis allows tax to be distinguished from penalties (and indeed criminal fines) without any appeal to the subjective attitude of the taxable person. Indeed, in the same way that Kelsen distinguishes between a demand for money from a gangster and a tax charge on the basis that the former has no authorising legal norm, whereas the latter does, a tax charge and a penalty/fine have quite different authorising norms (Kelsen 1967, 4–8). The different trigger conditions which impose a tax charge on the one hand and a penalty or fine on the other also mean that Hart's observation that the distinction is blurred for taxes which are disincentives and penalties/fines, or for fines which are 'cheerfully paid' by those who can afford them and treated as 'mere taxes' (Hart 2012, 39) does not undermine the bright line distinction between tax and penalties/fines made here.

TAX AND CIVIL PENALTIES

Distinguishing taxation from civil penalties is as easy as distinguishing taxes from monetary consideration for goods or services. A penalty arises by reason of doing a particular activity *of itself*. Put another way, there is a complete set of rules which prohibit behaviour. Another distinct rule will impose a penalty for breach. Contrast tax where the obligation to pay arises from the rules which identify the taxable person, the taxable activity, and the taxable amount. The taxable amount (and the tax charge) are distinct from any distinct enforcement jurisdiction which imposes separate obligations for breach of the obligation to pay the taxable amount. A tax charge arises on the exercise of prescriptive behaviour (enforcement is separate and after the imposition of the tax obligation itself).

For a penalty paid for breach of a (distinct) prohibition, there are no additional 'connecting factors' which are needed to attract liability. A parking fine arises because a driver has parked somewhere, or at a time at which, they ought not to have (they have breached a distinct rule which prohibited the relevant parking). No other condition need be satisfied. The fine is the exercise of a distinct enforcement for breach. Another way to put this is to observe that a fine (certainly a flat fine) cannot be described intelligibly as a 'taxable amount', having no rational connection to any attributes which define a taxable person or the manner of how a taxable activity is undertaken.

Consider a disincentive on the employment of child labour. How is such a disincentive to be categorised as either a tax or a penalty? The distinction is to be found in the archaeology of the monetary obligation. If the monetary obligation is imposed on a taxable person, with connecting factors to the taxing jurisdiction, who undertakes a taxable activity which produces a tax base (which is modified to increase the taxable amount by reference to the disincentivised component activity, the employment of a child) and the charge has a rational connection to the attributes of the taxable person and the taxable activity, the obligation is a 'tax'. And the charge is on a 'taxable amount'. It would equally be a tax if the employment of child labour were itself a deemed taxable activity and if there were connecting factors which must be satisfied for the employer to be a taxable person in addition to the employment of the child. However, if the monetary obligation is imposed by reason of employment of the child and nothing more, the obligation is a penalty. The obligation arises by reason of the relevant activity, nothing more.

The United States Supreme Court had to address this very question in the context of a charge on employers (of 10 per cent on their net profits for a year) if the employers were discovered to employ children under the age of 14, holding that such a charge (described as a 'Tax on the Employment of Child Labor' in the Revenue Act of February, 24, 1919, Title XII, enacted by Congress) was, in fact, not a 'tax' at all but a penalty which could only be imposed by the State of North Carolina and not a 'tax' which could be imposed by Congress. The lack of apportionment based on frequency or duration and the relevance of knowledge (there was no obligation if the employer reasonably believed that the child was over 14) were both held to be relevant in reaching this decision: *Bailey v Drexel Furniture Co*, 259 US 20 (1922) at 35 (per Taft CJ).

At first sight, this approach seems wrong. While a charge which arises irrespective of what activity an employer did and whether that activity was a taxable activity or not is clearly a penalty (not a tax), the charge in *Bailey* arose on 'net profits' of a taxable activity undertaken by a taxable person. These 'net profits' represented the product of a tax computation of a taxable person's tax base. If there was no taxable activity, there would be no net (taxable) profits. So the charge seemingly might be viewed as a component part of the tax computation. But the Supreme Court's decision is correct. The requirement of *knowledge* of the child's age was otherwise foreign to the tax computation of the employer. A charge which arises by reason of knowledge or belief arises from a source different to the taxable activity and is not a 'tax'.

The distinction is fine but a real one. Is the intention of the relevant statutory provisions to increase a taxable amount, where the connecting factors to a taxing jurisdiction are relevant, or is the intention to penalise the employment of child labour by imposing the obligation to pay by reason of such employment of itself? The answer in *Bailey* was gleaned through scrutiny of the relevant legal material (in that case, the statutory provisions). This was sufficient to permit the relevant legal norm to be identified as 'there is a law that you should not knowingly employ children under 14, otherwise you will be subject to a monetary charge'. This formulation exposes the nature of the charge to be a penalty, not a tax. That the amount was computed by reference to net profits was irrelevant.

TAX AND CRIMINAL FINES

Taxation is distinguishable from criminal fines or penalties in the same way as from civil fines. Of course, tax law may acknowledge and disapprove of criminality or other legal disapproval of certain activities; so expenditure incurred for an illegal activity (eg, payment of a parking fine) is not a deductible expense from the taxable profits of a trade: *CIR v Alexander von Glehn* [1920] 12 TC 232. But this observation does not affect the proposition that criminality and a tax liability arise from two separate sets of legal norms and may thus arise in respect of the same act-situation.

A tax charge which arises from the exercise of prescriptive jurisdiction which yields a taxable amount is different to a criminal fine which arises on the enforcement of a prohibition which is criminalised. Different legal and extra-legal consequences may well flow from the imposition of a criminal fine to those of a civil penalty, or a tax charge; the stamp of a criminal conviction impressed upon a criminal fine may well have different consequences for job prospects to those of a civil penalty or an additional tax charge; a guest at a dinner party may well be ostracised if he is convicted of employing child labour, as opposed to paying additional tax. However, no appeal to these legal or extra-legal considerations is needed to distinguish civil fines or criminal fines from tax charges: the former are imposed for the breach of a prohibition; the latter arises as an exercise of prescriptive jurisdiction, not the breach of any rule at all.

The same is true of monies recovered because a person obtained those monies through unlawful means, say fraud. An action for the recovery of monies obtained through alleged fraud, where the monies were paid by a tax authority to a person who made alleged fraudulent representations, is not an action for the recovery of 'tax'. In *Skatteforvaltiningen (The Danish Customs and Tax Authority) v Solo Capital Partners LLP* [2022] EWCA Civ 234 ('*Skat CA*'), the Danish tax authority had paid monies to persons who claimed tax payments on the basis that they were entitled to these payments because of certain tax reliefs due to shareholders of a company. The Court of Appeal held that these monies were not 'tax' (and thus outside the scope of the rule in *Government of India v Taylor* [1955] AC 491 that foreign revenue debts were unenforceable within the UK). Put short, the action was for the recovery of monies allegedly fraudulently obtained (because the monies had been paid to persons who, the Danish tax authority asserted, never had any shares in the relevant companies). There was no enforcement of a claim to 'tax' (see [126]–[153], especially [128] and [143], (per Sir Julian Flaux C)). This approach was endorsed by the Supreme Court in *Skatteforvaltningen (The Danish Customs and Tax Authority) v Solo Capital Partners LLP* [2023] UKSC 40 ('*Skat SC*') at [37]–[52] (especially at [43]), per Lord Lloyd Jones.

This approach and conclusion are clearly correct. The action was not brought on the basis that the payee-debtor was a 'taxable person' with some 'connecting factor' to the taxing authority (Denmark). There was, therefore, no 'taxable activity' and no 'taxable amount' relevant to this claim (although the underlying company did in fact exist and did carry on a taxable activity, there was no connection between the company and the defendants who fraudulently claimed to be shareholders in that company). There was an (alleged) unlawful activity (the allegedly fraudulent claim for monies) which was of itself subject to a remedy (repayment). To rephrase, the fact that the alleged unlawful claim was made by submitting a tax computation to a taxing authority does not mean that a claim for repayment of those monies is a claim for 'tax', any more than would, say, any other fraudulent claim made by submitting a false document to another party with a view to obtaining a benefit. It might also be said that the defendants had received a 'relief' having paid no relevant tax. Accordingly, the claim to clawback an allegedly wrongly claimed 'relief' could not be said to be 'tax' as it is the exact opposite: a tax reduction mechanism.

The basis for the distinction of a tax charge from both civil penalties and criminal fines is more solid than some alternative bases of distinction. For example, any distinction drawn between these two areas of law by reference to their respective effects on behaviour and autonomy, or their respective purposes is inadequate. Civil penalties, criminal fines and taxation may all have the same purpose (to disincentivise certain behaviours) and do the same work. This observation merely reinforces the nature of taxation (and indeed civil penalties and criminal fines) as a legal mode, which may serve different functions (which may, in turn, be fulfilled in any one of several ways).

A distinction based on the purpose of criminal fines, which seeks to contrast those to the purpose of taxation, fares no better. It has been said that, unlike criminal law, taxation is not a form of retribution or a utilitarian welfare-consequentialist form of punishment. Tax, it is said, does not deprive citizens of their normal rights and does not amount to an interference with the autonomy of an individual which is why there is, in the context of tax, no equivalent of the presumption against the criminalisation of a particular activity: Rawls 1969, 111–12. But a detriment applied to an individual as a disincentive affects the individual's autonomy whatever the nature of the legal mode in question. The only purpose of using any legal mode as a disincentive is to dissuade a particular individual from pursuing a particular course of action he would otherwise have undertaken. The imposition of the disincentive may be seen as a 'punishment', which is identical in nature, albeit not in strength or effect, whether the disincentive is a tax charge, civil penalty or a criminal fine. It follows that an appeal to the effect of a measure upon behaviour and autonomy will not distinguish taxation from a criminal fine.

Neither is an appeal to the 'harm principle' a convincing basis for distinguishing taxation from criminal fines. Feinberg (1987, 26) summarises the harm principle as follows:

> It is always a good reason in support of penal legislation that it would be effective in preventing (eliminating, reducing) harm to persons other than the actor (the one prohibited from acting) and there is no other means that is equally effective at no greater cost to other values.

The very notion of tax as a disincentive pre-supposes that the disincentivised activity is causing 'harm', however defined. Criminalisation reflects a choice of sanction for the breach of a prior legal norm. But that sanction could just as well be a tax charge or a civil penalty, without disturbing any justification for imposing detriment by reference to the harm principle, although with tax the harm principle often extends to self-harm (see, for example, the sugar tax). The harm principle, in asking whether a criminalised act is harmful, may equally ask, of that same harmful, prohibited act, whether a breach of that legal norm should be 'punished' by a charge to tax or a civil penalty. It is accepted, however, that for some harmful acts a tax will not be appropriate punishment (eg for criminal property damage). The harm principle cannot, therefore, distinguish taxation from a criminal fine.

On the other hand, an appreciation of the different trigger conditions and the nature of the jurisdiction which causes a tax charge to arise, on the one hand, and the nature of the enforcement jurisdiction for (in one way or another) breach of a prohibition on the other, readily distinguishes tax obligation from civil penalties and criminal fines.

TAX AND TORTIOUS DAMAGES

The same analysis may validly be applied to distinguish taxation from damages for tortious acts, at least for negligence. Of course, such damages are intuitively nothing like tax obligations, but a tax applied as a disincentive to dangerous activity which might harm others, say the sale of fireworks, may have a similar regulatory object and effect to the tort of negligence as applied to the use of fireworks, so an exercise to distinguish between the two is worthwhile. This is straightforward. An obligation to pay damages because one has failed to reach a standard of care towards someone to whom one has a duty of care is far away from an obligation to pay monies in respect of a taxable activity because the person undertaking it has connecting factors to a taxing jurisdiction. Different legal norms underpin damages which arise from the tort of negligence (those which inform a duty of care, a standard of care, causation, foreseeability remoteness), and loss and monies payable as a tax obligation (what are the putative taxable activities and what legitimates connecting factors). Loss also plays a role in distinguishing tax from tortious damages. Whilst some taxes might be explained by referenced to an assumed loss caused by the taxable activity, for tortious damages to arise the loss needs to be crystallised and proved.

CONCLUSIONS

Taxation has completely different trigger conditions from the other monetary obligations which have been considered (and these other monetary obligations have completely different trigger conditions from each other). The underlying norms which justify each of taxation, the enforcement of an obligation to pay consideration for goods or services ('user fees'), civil penalties and criminal fines are also all different from each other. The legitimacy of connecting factors of a person who undertakes a putative taxable activity by reference to that person's tax residence or the location of the taxable activity is informed by quite different considerations from those which inform whether a bargain should be kept, or whether an activity of itself, without more, should be sanctioned with either a civil penalty or a criminal conviction.

Thus, the individuation of taxation, by reference to the notions of the connecting factors (the trigger conditions) discussed in chapter one which make the undertaking of a putative taxable activity a taxable activity, provides a straightforward basis for positively identifying a tax charge, as well as a straightforward basis for distinguishing taxation from 'user fees', civil penalties, criminal fines and tortious damages.

5. 'CAPACITY' RATHER THAN 'NORM'

The approach taken above identifies taxation by reference to the formal requirements (the trigger conditions) which attract a particular obligation and the substance of the legal norms which underpin them. The language of 'capacity' also distinguishes a tax liability from other money debts. A person who is within the taxing jurisdiction of a tax-imposing body and triggers the application of charging provisions which establish the tax base for a particular tax is a 'taxpayer' and owes an obligation to the taxing authority in their capacity as a 'taxpayer'.

By contrast, in the case of a person liable to pay a consideration for goods or services, that person has the capacity of an 'acquirer'. In the case of a civil penalty, a person has a capacity of a person who has 'done something', no more, no less. The same is true for an 'offender': it is just that the sanction is criminal, not civil. Consideration of strict liability is redundant. Strict liability merely removes the need for any subjective intent for the imposition of either a civil penalty or criminal fine. The differences of the trigger conditions from those which attract a tax charge remain.

So the capacities of 'taxable person', 'acquirer of goods or services', 'wrongdoer' (who has done something specific which attracts a civil penalty), 'offender' (who has done something which attracts a criminal fine) and 'tortfeasor' are not merely different labels which self-servingly distinguish different types of payment without a sound juristic analytical frame. Rather, the distinctions made on the basis of 'capacity' reflect the different content of the conditions which give rise to different types of obligation.

Expressed in the language of capacity, a liability to taxation may be expressed as 'a liability to pay money for the sole reason of being a "taxable person" who has undertaken a taxable activity and has sufficient connecting factors to a taxing jurisdiction'. This is in contradistinction to the other capacities here. Capacity therefore provides an alternative method of distinguishing different species of monetary liability.

6. AUTHORITY

What of authority? If binding authority contradicts the model of a 'tax' charge in chapter one, the model would have to be revisited. There are no cases where the ratio contradicts the analysis in this work. Some cases deal with a very specific question but do not confront the central nature of a 'tax' charge. Other cases yield obiter observations on the nature of 'tax' without providing any analytical foundation, whilst a third category of cases are cases on whether a particular body had the vires to impose a charge, assuming that any ultra vires charge was (again without analytical foundation) a 'tax', making these latter cases of very little juristic value (at least on the question of 'what is a tax') indeed.

There are only five authorities which address the notion of 'tax' as part of the ratio: *Brewster v Kidgill* (1687) 88 ER 1239; *Baker v Greenhill* (1842) 114 ER 443; *IRC v Oce van der Grinten* [2000] STC 551; *Metal Industries (Salvage) Ltd v Owners of the ST Harle* [1962] SLT 114; and *Aston Cantlow* (CA).

The first four of these are mundane. *Brewster* confirms that the central case of a tax is a statutory ('parliamentary') tax destined for use by the Crown, but expressly leaves room for charges of other kinds. *Baker* is nothing more than authority for the proposition that, in the context of a lease, a common law liability which is codified does not become a 'Parliamentary tax' (at 470). *Oce van der Grinten* is authority for the unexceptionable proposition that, to the extent that a liability to a specific tax, Advance Corporation Tax, in the hands of a dividend-paying UK company under the UK tax code which might have been reduced by a tax credit is in fact *not* so reduced, the charge that remains is 'in substance' a tax: at 960 per Jacob J. At first blush, the Outer House in Scotland in *Metal Industries* appears to apply the four-stage *Lawson* test discussed above; in fact, however, Lord Cameron expressly reserved his position as to whether the charges were 'taxes' or 'charges or impositions of like nature' (at 116).

These cases, although they address the notion of 'tax' as part of their respective ratios, say virtually nothing about the juristic attributes of a liability to tax. None is inconsistent in its ratio with the model discussed in chapter one or with the individuated notion of taxation set out in this chapter. All these cases concerned a monetary non-proprietary obligation. None of these cases confines the notion of taxation to a demand by a public body or to one which applies monies for public purposes. The UK Supreme Court's decision in *Skat SC* unsurprisingly did not contribute further to the case law: the issue in *Skat SC* was framed as to whether a claim is *not* a tax claim (and cannot be since it has no relevance to any person's tax computation), rather than what tax *is*.

Further authorities that offer general obiter observations as to the nature of taxation, none which engage directly with the specific juristic character of taxation, are *Coltness Iron Company v Black* [1881] 1 TC 287; *Congreve v Home Office* [1976] QB 629 (not concerning the meaning of 'tax' at all, but rather licence fees); and *Daymond v South West Water Authority* (on the correct analysis of water charges). In the last of these, the minority's analysis corresponded exactly to the individuated conception of a 'tax' set out in this chapter; the majority, however, did not, and all members of the House of Lords appear to have assumed (without this forming any express ratio) 'tax' to be the imposition of a monetary obligation where the only relevant feature is that the obligation is not a function of goods or services received. Although not inconsistent with the model in chapter one, this is incomplete for the reasons canvassed above.

There are also authorities in which the only question was whether a public body had vires to impose an obligation to pay or not, rather than as to the positive nature of a 'tax' charge: *Bowles v Bank of England* [1913] 1 Ch 57 (tax cannot be levied without legislative authority); *Ormond*

Investment Company v Betts [1928] 13 TC 400, 426 (incorrect analogy between taxes, criminal fines and penalties); *Scott v Russell* [1948] AC 422 (need for clear authority to impose a tax); *Attorney-General v Wilts United Dairies* (1927) 37 TLR 884 (no vires to charge a licence fee for milk distribution). All these cases simply treat 'tax' as the antonym of the payment authorised by the relevant statute and thus have nothing positively to say on the juristic definition of tax. But as such, the cases in this category are not inconsistent with the model in chapter one.

Aston Cantlow (CA) squarely does address the question of 'what is a tax'. The decision of the English Court of Appeal confirms in this case that, at least for the purposes of the Human Rights Act 1998 (HRA), taxation is a monetary liability (not a property liability), that taxation may arise from a common law (not legislative) source and that there is no special notion of 'public' or government purpose inherent in the juristic notion of taxation.

Freehold owners of English real property assumed (by reason of ownership) the capacity of rectors of the rectory of the parish of Aston Cantlow and the liability to the Parochial Church Council (PCC) to meet the costs of repair of the parish church chancel. The freeholders and the land they owned was 'shorn of any connection' to the church or the rectory ([45], [51]). The liability was imposed by common law, not statute ([12], [37]), travelled with the land ([15], [16]) and indeed was expressly provided for in the conveyance to the owners ([21]). A preliminary point is that the relevant obligation arose without any consent on the part of the obligor; the obligor did not bargain to assume this obligation in consideration of anything delivered by the payee. A common law obligation imposed absent any consent of the payor fits into the model discussed in chapter one.

The entirety of the Court of Appeal's analysis of the meaning of 'tax' is contained at [40]. The status of the PCC as a 'public body' was addressed only to ascertain whether the HRA was engaged, nothing else. The touchstone of categorisation of the liability as a 'tax' was that 'the legal liability [was] ... a personal liability [albeit] deriving from a legal relationship with land ..., analogous to council tax ... The levy is upon [the freeholders'] personal funds. Their ownership of [the real property conveyed to them, subject to the liability for repairs expressed in the relevant conveyance], while it is the source of their liability, is undisturbed.' The Court of Appeal considered the liability as 'quite different from that in which an outright owner of property finds that his ownership is entrenched upon by some outside intervention in the form of taxation'.

The Court of Appeal thus distinguishes between a liability *qua* land-owner and a personal liability, imposed by 'outside intervention'. This is consistent with the model in chapter one. To be sure, there was no reference to any connecting factor (to the enforcing church), or to any putative or actual taxable activity, although implicitly this must be, in both cases, the ownership of the relevant property (this is what makes the actual conclusion of the court problematic: see below). There was no reference to the legislative scheme of HRA 1998, nor to any HRA 1998 or ECHR case law on 'tax', so the Court of Appeal's analysis of what is a 'tax' is not confined to the corners of HRA 1998. The categorisation by the Court of Appeal of the liability for chancel repairs as a 'tax' was left untouched by the House of Lords (as a matter of ratio). The obiter dicta of Lord Hope, Lord Hobhouse and Lord Scott (discussed below) do not deprive the Court of Appeal's judgment on this point of its status as binding authority. Neither the House of Lords collectively, nor any individual judge suggested that their respective (not identical) obiter observations were anything other than exactly that.

While the Court of Appeal's general analysis in *Aston Cantlow* (CA) is correct in principle, the Court of Appeal erred in applying its analysis in categorising the chancel repair liability as a tax. This is not because the liability arose at common law (as discussed above), or because it was purely functional, or because of the relevance of the concepts of 'public body', 'public interest' or 'public purpose', but because closer analysis reveals that the liability does not answer to the juristic notion of a tax set out in the model discussed in chapter one or the principles which indi-viduate tax discussed in this chapter.

The difficulty is that the putative taxable activity (namely, holding the freehold) was itself, without more, constitutive of the obligation to pay; there were no additional tax connecting factors to fix the obliga-tion to pay. The crucial analytical ingredient of a tax connecting factor to categorise a person as a taxable person was wholly absent. It follows that the obligation could not be a tax. The same conclusion is suggested by a capacity analysis: the freeholders' liability, though purely personal, was *qua* freeholder alone. The chancel repair liability was therefore not a tax and should more closely be analogised to a restrictive covenant (*Aston Cantlow* (HL) at [69] (per Lord Hope), [171] (per Lord Rodger)) or, borrowing from Scots law (prior to 2000), feu duties (that is, an incident of landholding).

Indeed, there is a risk that the Court of Appeal's classification of the chancel repair liability as a tax was an instance of the common but misguided tendency to characterise tax purely in contradistinction to property. Indeed it is not obvious that council tax, referred to by the Court of Appeal, is indeed a 'tax', despite its name, any more than the 'rates' they replaced. There is no 'taxable activity', putative or otherwise. Rather the charge arises merely by occupying a particular building. This compulsory charge for occupation has the character of some sort of charge qua member of a community (literally a 'community charge') rather than that of a 'tax'.

On appeal to the House of Lords ([2003] UKHL 37), three of the five sitting members of the House of Lords addressed, in obiter dicta, the question whether the chancel repair liability was a 'tax'. For Lords Hope and Hobhouse, the central reason for rejecting the classification of the liability as a tax was that it had 'arise[n] under private law' (at [63]) or had 'been converted into [a] civil obligation' (at [92]). Without more, however, this reasoning is circular: it assumes that all tax obligations are somehow 'public' and, as Lord Scott pointed out at [131], rests on the false assumption that all civil obligations are private law ones.

Lord Scott reasoned on the alternative basis that the archaeology of the chancel repair liability was as a 'quid pro quo for the receipt of the tithe rent-charge' (see [133]). He did not specify the appropriate classification of the chancel repair obligation but his speech is most naturally read as categorising the liability as a *sui generis* civil obligation sitting outside of both private law and tax law. In further dicta, Lord Scott accepted that a common law obligation to pay tithes to the rector could 'reasonably be regarded as an obligation to pay a tax' (at [131]).

Whether a tithe in fact answers to the juristic definition of a tax set out in chapter one depends on the content of the liability and whether the obligee must have connecting factors to the obligee additional to being the occupant of land (if not, the obligation is not a 'tax'). In any event, what is most significant for present purposes is Lord Scott's endorsement of the proposition that an obligation arising at common law might properly be described as a 'tax' liability. This observation makes good the proposition that a tax need not be paid to or imposed by a public body, which is why the House of Lords' approach cannot be seen to disturb this proposition. In any event, Lord Scott's acknowledgement that a common law tithe might constitute a tax is obiter judicial acceptance that a 'common law tax' is not a contradiction in terms. This point was also made in *Air Caledonie* (at 467) and *Australian Tape Manufacturers Association* (at 501): 'it is not essential to the concept of a tax that the exaction should be done by a public authority' (per Mason CJ).

This survey of the domestic UK case law shows that the model in chapter one and the individuated notion of tax discussed in this chapter (a personal monetary obligation, which depends upon a person who undertakes a putative taxable activity who also has additional connecting factors to the taxing jurisdiction which are trigger conditions which must be satisfied to attract an obligation to pay) is not inconsistent with the conclusions (not always with the reasoning) of UK case law. This individuated notion of tax is also consistent with Australian authority, albeit not with Canadian authority, as demonstrated above.

7. CONCLUSION

Returning to the Henry VIII power in section 14 of the 2023 Act, it ought to be relatively straightforward to identify a prohibited tax, by contrast to a permitted penalty or fine. The touchstone is whether a person fixed with an obligation to pay attracts that obligation merely by doing something (penalty, or fine) of by doing something and in addition possessing additional connecting factors (which may be but need not be analogous to residence or source).

This chapter contends that tax law is itself a key idea. Tax law may be properly located as an area of law which is identifiable and coherent, despite its modal nature, and distinct from those other areas of law which may have an external relationship with tax provisions.

RESPONSES TO CHAPTER FOUR

PROFESSOR ANN MUMFORD, PROFESSOR OF TAXATION LAW, KING'S COLLEGE LONDON

When HLA Hart considered the definition of a tax, it was because he hoped to prove the fallacies of the command theory of law (Hart 2008, 6). If one agrees with the command theory of law, he argued, then one cannot tell the difference between a tax and a fine, when we know that these two phenomena are distinct, if also very difficult to distinguish – just look, Hart suggested, at the United States Supreme Court in the first half of the twentieth century (as Professor Ghosh does here), and its struggle to distinguish the terms. The distinction matters in American law, because whilst the US federal government is empowered by its constitution to tax in some circumstances, criminal law (at least traditionally) is left to the states. Does the definition of a tax matter in the UK, a (unitary, if one disregards devolution for the moment) parliamentary democracy? In some circumstances, as Professor Ghosh explains, it matters very much, especially if the United Kingdom is engaging with laws addressing taxation in other jurisdictions.

Within the context of UK law, however, the modal nature of the tax obligation has been revealed in earlier chapters as coherent, sometimes reliable and often predictable. The contribution of this book is that whilst much of the philosophical work considering taxation does not appreciate the juristic nature of a tax obligation, the model presented here takes tax law seriously. Whereas chapter six will pick up these issues in more detail, here, in chapter four, the fallacy of considering tax law narrowly is demonstrated. Take the example of tax incidence: this is not the point at which economists take lead of the discussion from the lawyers, who, having contributed to the analysis of whether an obligation exists, now exit the conversation. Quite the opposite, for, if an obligation is capable of being set off, then it is a personal obligation, and distinguishable from an obligation in property law. As the nature of the obligation is monetary, however, the taxpayer's personhood is irrelevant (as demonstrated by the key example of *Oram v Johnson* [1980] STC 222), and 'unattractively' so.

This is the point that Hart, the famed tax barrister, missed: he considered the definition of a tax from the perspective of how the person experiences it (is the experience one of punishment, taxation, deterrence? etc) Yet taxation, 'unattractively', does not always care about, or value, the person. The value of a person's own labour (as held in *Oram*) does not qualify as enhancement expenditure, as one's 'personal attributes cannot be monetised' (as the author explains) for taxation. The consequence of the monetary nature of taxation, thus, is the dilution of the importance of the (myriad) objectives of taxation to taxpayers. If taxation is 'only' about money, and not about me, then tax's power to punish or regulate me is lessened. This important chapter thus both finishes a conversation started by Hart, and extends Raz's individuation project to taxation law, which emerges with limitations, and clarity.

Author's response: Professor Mumford locates chapter four within what was an important debate between Hart and Kelsen (Hart 1961), where Hart accused Kelsen of failing to distinguish between a tax and a criminal fine because Kelsen thought that both were sanctions of the same type. But Kelsen's formulation can easily accommodate taxes and fines as 'sanctions' arising from very different legal sources. To see tax as arising from the exercise of prescriptive jurisdiction and a fine as arising from enforcement jurisdiction (because a separate law has been breached) means that the distinction is, as Professor Mumford explains, actually quite clear and that Hart was perhaps unfair in criticising Kelsen for failing to distinguish between the two. 'If one undertakes a taxable activity and has a sufficient connecting factor to a charge-imposing body, one must pay an amount of money computed on a 'taxable amount' [prescriptive jurisdiction], failing which there will be interest and (perhaps) penalties [enforcement jurisdiction]' is a quite different law to 'one must not undertake a particular activity [prescriptive jurisdiction] failing which one must pay money to a charge-imposing body [enforcement jurisdiction]', even when the two respective activities and the two amounts are identical.

NICOLA SHAW, GRAY'S INN TAX CHAMBERS, CHAIR
OF THE REVENUE BAR ASSOCIATION 2016–19

Tax law, as the name suggests, deals with the rules and regulations governing the imposition and collection of tax. It is, however, impossible to garner any real understanding as to the nature and singularity of tax law without first establishing a proper definition of its subject matter. As such, the question at the heart of this chapter, indeed at the heart of this book, is 'what is tax'? Identifying the purposes of, or justifications for, tax may provide us with an interesting backdrop and stimulate debate as to 'why' or 'when' tax should be charged but it does not assist us in answering the question of 'what' tax is.

As this chapter explains, what distinguishes tax law from other areas of the law is that it is concerned with unique concepts. The core components identified by the author which define what tax is – the 'taxable person', 'taxable amount' and 'taxable activity' – and which determine when tax law is engaged do not appear in other legal landscapes: whereas the law of tort is concerned with tortfeasors, tax law is concerned with the 'taxable person'; whereas the law of contract is concerned with damages for breach of contract, tax law is concerned with the 'taxable amount'; whereas the law of landlord and tenant is concerned with leasehold interests, tax law is concerned with 'taxable activities.

It can therefore be seen that defining the meaning of the word tax with a sufficient degree of precision and specificity reveals the uniqueness of tax law. It is the particularity of the core components that sets tax law apart. That is not to say that tax law can be viewed in isolation. The author's all-encompassing concept of 'taxable activity' reflects the omnipresence of tax in our daily lives – for example, through income taxes, sales taxes, property taxes, corporate taxes – which inevitably requires tax law to interface with other branches of the law – for example employment law, contract law, land law, company law. Nevertheless, tax law is its own mistress – a distinct and specialised area of law – notorious for its complexity and comprising an ever-evolving multitude of statutes, regulations and judicial decisions.

Focusing on the core components – the 'what', as opposed to the 'why' or the 'when' – not only reveals the nature of tax law but is vital to the practice and development of tax law. Like all forms of law, tax law concerns the interpretation and application of specified rules in a manner which ensures consistency, predictability and fairness. Given the many and varied rationales for tax – for example, to fund government activity or to incentivise (or disincentivise) certain behaviour – attempting to identify the 'why' or the 'when' is fraught with subjectivity; the professed 'purpose' is but a fig-leaf for the adjudicator's personal political proclivities.

Focusing on the 'what' not only reveals the common concepts and fundamental principles which permeate and underpin the law but allows us to see what would otherwise be regarded as a disparate and diverse collection of taxes as a rational and cohesive whole.

Author's response: Ms Shaw's response, focussing as it does on the 'what' and not the 'why' or 'when' of tax law, captures the essence of analytical jurisprudence generally and the approach of this chapter in particular. In particular any definition of 'tax' by reference to how a charge is perceived by the person on the receiving end of it is destined to fall into incoherence; the same imposition cannot be a 'tax' in the hands of one person but not another because, say, the former views its effect as a minor inconvenience (despite its status as a criminal fine), while the latter respects its legal status.

5

The Reprehensibility of 'Tax Avoidance'

1. INTRODUCTION

The key idea within tax law explored in this chapter is that the notion that 'tax avoidance' is reprehensible is an established legal norm of presumptive application of statutory construction. Of course, the anterior question is whether there is 'avoidance' in the first place, as it is only if there is 'avoidance' and not mere 'mitigation' that any such norm applies. As observed above and again in this chapter, the avoidance/mitigation distinction is an imprecise exercise. This chapter does not address what (precisely) is 'tax avoidance'. Not because this issue can be at all avoided but because it is properly located in chapter two, within the larger question of what is the correct approach in principle to the construction and application of tax provisions.

Before turning to a definition of tax avoidance and to a discussion of how its reprehensibility has gained the status of a legal norm, it is worth illustrating how it is that the courts treat tax avoidance as 'reprehensible'.

In *Bhaur & Ors v Equity First Trustees (Nevis) Ltd* [2023] STC 1012 ('*Bhaur*'), the taxpayers entered into an inheritance tax (IHT) avoidance scheme whereby their property business was transferred first to a UK company, then to a company in the British Virgin Islands, and finally to a trust in the British Virgin Islands for the benefit of the employees of the UK company, with the intention that the taxpayers' children would later be able to receive the business free of IHT. The scheme failed. The taxpayers applied to the court for the transfers to be set aside on the ground of mistake under the rubric set out in *Pitt v Holt* [2013] UKSC 26. That application's refusal by the High Court was upheld by the Court of Appeal for two reasons.

First, given the risks involved in artificial tax avoidance schemes, the taxpayers were to be taken as having run the risk of their own mistake: *Bhaur* at [84] (per Snowden LJ). This was also part of the reasoning in *Dukeries Healthcare Ltd v Bay Trust International Ltd* [2021] EWHC 2086 (Ch), at [91] (per Deputy Master Marsh), interpreting *Pitt v Holt* at [153]. Second, the fact that tax avoidance is a 'social evil' (because it imposes an unfair burden on taxpayers who do not undertake such schemes) was a powerful factor indicating that it would not be unconscionable to refuse equitable relief (*Bhaur* at [105]), tax avoidance having been the sole reason for the scheme (*Bhaur* at [102]–[104]). The reprehensibility of tax avoidance formed part of the ratio of the decision (*Bhaur* at [106]).

The purpose of this chapter is to place on a sound juristic footing the proposition, relied on in *Bhaur*, that the social attitude that 'tax avoidance is reprehensible' has legal effect. This chapter also addresses how tax avoidance's reprehensibility is, in some cases, itself a legal norm, not merely a social attitude. To make these propositions good, it is necessary: (1) to define tax avoidance, (2) to consider what differentiates legal norms from social (or extra-legal) norms and (3) to show that tax avoidance's reprehensibility now constitutes both social attitude capable of legal effect and itself a legal norm. This chapter also considers whether that latter legal norm is of presumptive general application; that is, it applies unless excluded.

2. TAX AVOIDANCE, TAX MITIGATION AND TAX EVASION

As was observed in chapter one, a taxable person engages in 'tax avoidance' when they do something to prevent a tax obligation from arising at all, in a manner which was not intended by the 'reasonable' legislature (the test in *R (Project for the Recognition of Children as British Citizens) v Secretary of State for the Home Department* [2022] UKSC 3 ('*PRCBC*')). So, one way or another, a taxpayer engaged in tax avoidance seeks to escape or defer a tax charge on otherwise taxable amounts or to obtain deductions from taxable amounts by effecting transactions for that very purpose (even if also for other, non-avoidance purposes). Tax mitigation, by contrast, is the reduction or extinction of a tax obligation in a manner invited by Parliament (either expressly or by reasonably implication, on the reasonable legislature test). Tax evasion is the illegitimate avoidance of a crystallised tax obligation.

Any distinction between avoidance and mitigation cannot be made glibly (see the discussion in chapter one). It will be the very essence of any dispute between a taxpayer and HMRC in a tax avoidance case and involve the most anxious scrutiny by the courts. 'Tax avoidance' means what a court gleans from the relevant statute it means. This observation positively begs the question as to how a court goes about answering the critical prior question as to whether there is 'avoidance' which triggers any presumptive anti-avoidance norm. Any answer is necessarily imprecise (and to that extent unsatisfactory); the answer depends on the terms of the statute, its object and whether that object reasonably includes the result sought by the taxpayer. It is only if the answer to the last question is 'no', that any anti-avoidance norm of construction applies.

The answer will vary from statute to statute. It is rare for a statute to provide a clear steer on whether a particular course of action is 'avoidance' or 'mitigation', especially where that course of action might have stemmed from a mixture of motives, both tax-driven (to secure some sort of tax benefit) and non-tax. A linguistic distinction between 'avoidance' and 'mitigation' simply begs the question as to which term encompasses what. But if a court holds that there is 'avoidance', the question arises as to whether, if the statute is silent, there is any legal presumptive anti-avoidance norm of construction which is to be applied to frustrate that 'avoidance' (the answer is 'yes'). It is this latter issue which is examined here.

3. LEGAL NORMS AND SOCIAL NORMS

Both social norms and legal norms have legal effects, in different ways. A working distinction between the legal effect of social and legal norms can be drawn as follows.

SOCIAL NORMS

A social attitude or norm can only have an indirect legal effect and even then have application only where these meet access conditions such as to inform the application of legal norms. Laying aside for the moment the difficulty of whose social norms are identified as relevant and how they are identified, a social norm can only have legal effect by informing the construction and application of a legal norm (say a statutory provision) and only then if the legal norm properly accommodates the input of the social norm.

A possible example is the 'always speaking' principle discussed in chapter two: in settling the meaning of a contested provision, it is appropriate to take into account changing social attitudes (so that, for example, what is 'cruel and unusual' in the twenty-first century may bear little resemblance to the same in the seventeenth: *R (Quintavalle) v Secretary of State for Health* [2003] UKHL 13, [9] (per Lord Bingham of Cornhill)).

In the law, social attitudes are only given effect through the medium of a legal norm, for example a principle of statutory interpretation. So before social norms can have juridical consequences, they must 'plug in' to the legal material within the legal system.

An illustration of the problematic consequences of applying social norms directly is the much-criticised decision of the House of Lords in *Roberts v Hopwood Poplar Council* [1925] AC 578. The council was entitled to set the wages of its employees 'as it thinks fit' and adopted a policy of equal pay regardless of sex. The House of Lords held that this was unlawful because the policy was an 'improper purpose' which was outside the council's jurisdiction. Lord Atkinson held (at 594):

> The council would, in my view, fail in their duty if, in administering funds which did not belong to their members alone, they put aside all these aids to the ascertainment of what was just and reasonable remuneration to give for the services rendered to them, and allowed themselves to be guided in preference by some eccentric principles of socialistic philanthropy, or by a feminist ambition to secure the equality of the sexes in the matter of wages in the world of labour.

In substance, the House of Lords in appears to have treated social attitudes in respect of equal pay as determinative. It is this that has provoked criticism of *Roberts v Hopwood* as 'one of the most outspoken political judgments ever to come from their Lordships' (Griffith 1993) and as an instance of 'judicial fallibility' (King 2008, 413) or of 'the common law … going backwards' (Sedley 2015, 31–32).

While the incongruity of *Roberts v Hopwood* with prevailing social attitudes today throws this into sharp relief, the decision's fundamental error from a juristic perspective is not the content of the social views that were applied (such criticism is social and political rather than legal), but rather the application of those views without regard for whether they had been or could be translated into legal norms. The House of Lords nowhere explains where the antipathy to equal pay came from as a relevant legal consideration to identify whether the policy was 'proper' or not. This failure to identify the source (or justification) for this alleged social norm was amplified by the failure to identify how it was accommodated into a legal assessment of what is, or is not, a 'proper' policy for a council to pursue.

In other words, the House of Lords did not explain which legal norm accommodated the anti-equal pay social norm and simply equated 'gender equality' as legally 'improper' because gender inequality was the prevalent social norm. By skipping the intermediate step of setting out the relevant legal material which accommodated the (prevalent) social discriminatory attitude, the House of Lords fell into error. This criticism does not impose today's attitudes on the House of Lords of the 1920s. It is a criticism of legal methodology. Of course, *Roberts v Hopwood* would be decided differently today, precisely because any challenge to the lawfulness of a wage policy that sought to eliminate discrimination would be decided by reference to mediating common law and statutory legal norms such as *Wednesbury* review, the principle of legality or the public sector equality duty, so that not only would such a policy be lawful, it would also most likely be mandatory.

Social norms are analogous to principles of construction of statutory provisions. The crucial point is that it is never sufficient to appeal to prevailing social attitudes of themselves. If a social norm is to have juridical effect, its translation into or through a legal norm is indispensable. Though discussions of 'canons of construction' are often unhelpfully vague or generic, principles of interpretation are a major medium through which both legal and social norms are given indirect legal effect. The attribution of an intention consistent with principle to the reasonable legislature (stage 2(b) in the process outlined in chapter two), through vehicles including the 'always speaking' principle, will often enable the courts to adopt a construction of a statute consistent with prevailing social attitudes.

To prevent this principle's transformation into a *carte blanche* for the application of extra-legal norms, the courts have affirmed the primacy of the words read in their context (stage 1 of the exercise of statutory construction discussed in chapter two). Accordance with the statutory text therefore imposes an access condition for the legal implementation of social norms. Given the prevalence of statute as a source for tax law, this will prove to be central to the analysis below of the transformation of tax avoidance's reprehensibility into a legal norm.

LEGAL NORMS

By contrast to social norms, legal norms are themselves legal material, which form part of the internal workings of the law. They provide the content of legal rules and/or govern the relationship between legal rules. Statutory provisions, case law, canons of construction and so forth are examples. Legal norms may arise and take their content from other legal norms. So, although the Human Rights Act 1998 does not have horizontal effect, Article 8 of the European Convention on Human Rights may inform private law duties of confidence amongst private persons: *Campbell v Mirror Group Newspapers* [2004] UKHL 22. And whereas a legal norm may be given effect directly (such as a statutory provision) or indirectly (say a canon of construction or general presumption, for example, against retrospective application of a statute), its application is automatic, in that on each and every occasion a given set of legal facts will fall within its scope (so both the statutory provision and the presumption against retrospectivity will operate to those legal facts). The outcome will always be subject to the applicable legal norms.

4. TAX AVOIDANCE'S REPREHENSIBILITY AS A SOCIAL OR EXTRA-LEGAL NORM

There is no doubt that social attitudes towards tax avoidance have hardened over the last century. The traditional view is that, until the 1970s, permissive attitudes towards tax avoidance prevailed; provided that the line separating avoidance from evasion was not crossed, taxpayers could properly do as they pleased to reduce their tax liabilities: see Snape 2019, 223–44; Aaronson 2016. This view was classically set out in *IRC v Duke of Westminster* [1936] AC 1, in which Lord Tomlin famously affirmed the right of taxpayers to reduce their liabilities by any lawful means: 'Every man is entitled if he can to order his affairs so that the tax attaching under the appropriate Acts is less than it otherwise would be' (at 19). By contrast, tax avoidance today is regarded as a social evil by politicians, by the public at large, and by the courts: see, for example, BBC News 2012; Wintour and Syal 2012.

Tax avoidance's description in *Bhaur* as a 'social evil' is not isolated, or recent. In *Matrix Securities Ltd v IRC* [1994] 1 All ER 769, Lord Templeman described the scheme in issue as 'designed to plunder the Treasury' (at 780); and in *Mayes v Revenue & Customs Commissioners* [2011] STC 1269, both Thomas and Toulson LJJ expressed their reluctance in finding that an aggressive avoidance scheme was effective, observing respectively that the taxpayers had 'received benefits that cannot possibly have been intended and which must be paid for by other taxpayers' (at 1292 (per Thomas LJ)), resulting in 'a windfall which Parliament cannot have foreseen or intended' (per Toulson LJ).

While judicial observations acknowledge changes in attitude (see, for example, Lord Diplock in *IRC v Burmah Oil* [1982] STC 30, at 32), it is an oversimplification to draw an absolute distinction between the approaches of the past and present. As early as the 1940s, the Court of Appeal noted that 'Parliament has regarded as improper attempts by individuals to shirk their fair share of fiscal responsibility': *Sassoon v Commissioner of Inland Revenue* [1942] 25 TC 154, 156 (per Scott LJ). The magnitude of the shift in social attitudes is therefore arguable. On any view, however, the change is a real one that can be observed not only through the law reports but also through public opinion polling (see YouGov's surveys on 'Tax Avoidance and Tax Evasion' (YouGov 2017)) and institutional attitudes (see the OECD's work on 'aggressive tax planning').

5. TAX AVOIDANCE'S REPREHENSIBILITY AS A STRONG GENERAL LEGAL NORM

There are two ways in which the courts have encoded tax avoidance's reprehensibility as a legal norm. First, by appealing to the reprehensible nature of tax avoidance as a social norm plugged into legal norms which accommodate this attitude. Second, by recognising such reprehensibility as a legal norm of general application in its own right.

ACCOMMODATION AS A SOCIAL ATTITUDE

The first approach appears in the line of cases to which *Bhaur* belongs, where a hostility to tax avoidance as a social attitude clothes the tax avoider with the attributes of a 'risk-runner', which, in turn, has implications for the grant or refusal of discretionary remedies (the legal norm into which the social attitude plugs). The Supreme Court in *Pitt v Holt*, revisiting the conditions under which voluntary dispositions can be rescinded for mistake, held (at [122]) that a causative mistake of sufficient gravity was required. Lord Walker observed, obiter, that the court may refuse relief in cases of artificial tax avoidance (at [135]):

> In some cases of artificial tax avoidance the court might think it right to refuse relief, either on the ground that such claimants, acting on supposedly expert advice, must be taken to have accepted the risk that the scheme would prove ineffective, or on the ground that discretionary relief should be refused on grounds of public policy. Since the seminal decision of the House of Lords in *WT Ramsay Ltd v IRC* [1982] AC 300 there has been an increasingly strong and general recognition that artificial tax avoidance is a social evil which puts an unfair burden on the shoulders of those who do not adopt such measures.

Lord Walker's reference to alternative bases for the refusal has given rise to two interpretations of this passage.

First, that, in determining whether a mistake is so grave that it would be unconscionable to leave it uncorrected, the court will consider the reprehensibility of tax avoidance directly (*Bhaur* at [105]). Here, the social norm of tax avoidance's reprehensibility is admitted to legal reasoning through the gateway of 'unconscionability'.

Second, that taxpayers engaging in artificial tax avoidance are risk-runners, and therefore not causally mistaken at all (*Bhaur* at [84] (per Snowden LJ); *Dukeries Healthcare Ltd v Bay Trust International Ltd* [2021] EWHC 2086 (Ch), at [91] (per Deputy Master Marsh)). The gateway, on this view, is the concept of risk-running within the law of mistaken transfers. This second approach 'deems' the risk-running even where there may be no such risk-running in fact.

On either view, the reprehensibility of tax avoidance as a social attitude is legally relevant via the legal norms governing judicial discretion on remedies. What is critical to this application of a judicial hostility towards tax avoidance is that the relevant legal norm (a statutory provision, or judicial discretion) must be sufficiently elastic to accommodate this social attitude (so a term like 'reasonable' may well accommodate changing social attitudes, whereas 'feu duty' will not). Otherwise a court, in applying a social attitude – here, hostility towards tax avoidance – would fall into the *Roberts v Hopwood* error identified above. And equally a court must identify why a particular transaction is 'avoidance' rather than 'mitigation' in relation to a particular statute.

THE EMERGENCE OF A GENERAL LEGAL NORM: *UBS*

The second mechanism through which tax avoidance's reprehensibility has been elevated to the status of a legal norm is the approach to 'purposive' construction in the line of anti-avoidance case law, often referred to as 'the *Ramsay* principle'. This takes its name from *WT Ramsay Ltd v IRC* [1981] STC 174, generally accepted as the first in the line of cases which expressly adopted a highly purposive approach to the construction of tax provisions. In this context, the proposition that tax avoidance is reprehensible has become a strong legal norm of general application. This approach has been extended significantly in *UBS AG v HMRC* [2016] UKSC 13 ('*UBS*').

The text-principle-authority approach set out in chapter two to statutory construction permits (mandates) that once the relevant provision is identified, its textual meaning is a function of 'principle', which, in this context, means the application of legal norms.

(1) *Pre-UBS: a provision-by-provision approach.* Prior to *UBS*, the text-principle-authority approach was exhaustively captured in the formulation of 'the ultimate question [of] ... whether the relevant statutory provisions, construed purposively, were intended to apply to the transaction, viewed realistically' (*Collector of Stamp Revenue v Arrowtown Assets Ltd* [2003] HKCFA 46 per Ribeiro PJ, at [35]; approved by the House of Lords in *Barclays Mercantile Business Finance Ltd v Mawson* [2005] STC 1, at [36]–[38]).

This is a mere application of the usual approach to legislative intent, identified on a provision-by-provision basis. There is no particular identification of 'tax avoidance' in any generic sense a something to be frustrated. The 'realistic' description of transactions simply means the most 'accurate' description of the relevant steps in the context of the tax in the relevant statute, ignoring camouflage and irrelevant distractions. So where the sale of an investment asset (shares in a company) from A to B is taxable to CGT but for various reasons a sale by A to C (A's wholly owned subsidiary) and then a sale by C to B is not taxable, a 'realistic' view of the transaction is a 'disposal' (which was the statutory provision being construed) by A to B, where it was A and B who had negotiated the sale and the price and where the C-B sale was always going to take place from the moment that A sold the shares to C. The A-C-B transactions were an irrelevance in these particular circumstances: *Furniss v Dawson* [1984] STC 153.

What is irrelevant in one statutory context may be relevant in another statutory context. The question will be whether, in a particular statutory context, particular features of a transaction are relevant or not: *UBS* at [68] (per Lord Reed). This is not always (or often) a simple exercise. The very issue in avoidance litigation may well be what is the object of the statute in question and what, therefore is 'relevant'. Lord Fraser, in *Furniss v Dawson* (at 155), adopted (like Lord Wilberforce before him in *Ramsay* supra, at 180) the useful terminology of 'the relevant transaction' being identified (here the A-B transaction, ignoring the commercially irrelevant A-C-B leg), thus focussing scrutiny on the questions of who are the 'relevant' (commercially 'true') parties, subject matter and consideration in the transaction, where 'relevance' is gleaned from the purpose of the statutory provisions being applied. In the context of CGT, what is 'relevant' is who is making a disposal of what and for what price: intermediaries inserted for CGT avoidance purposes who play no commercial role are irrelevant.

The terminology of 'the relevant transaction' was resurrected in *Schofield v HMRC* [2012] STC 2019, at [26], [39] (per Sir Andrew Morritt C). The identification of the statutory provisions and the interrogation of their text is stage 1 of the interpretation process set out in chapter two. The application of any presumption that tax-avoidance is reprehensible is an application of stage 2 (as a function of the legislature's intention as to how the provisions are supposed to work) which seeks to ascertain which of a number of competing textual meanings is the one which accords with legislative intent (principle).

This provision-by-provision approach to tax avoidance as an application of the general principle that statutes are to be interpreted purposively by reference to legislative intent is of long standing: *IRC v McGuckian* [1997] STC 908, at 916 (per Lord Steyn). It requires the identification of a particular statutory provision and its interrogation to decide which of the candidate linguistic meanings is correct in principle (bearing in mind the legislature's intention). So courts have had to grapple with whether the proceeds of the sale of a right to a dividend, where the proceeds were funded by the dividend payment to the assignee were 'income' in the hands of the assignor, for the purposes of anti-avoidance provisions which applied to 'income' ('yes': *IRC v McGuckian*); whether the acquirer of gilts who sold (and was always going to sell) those same gilts back to the seller was 'entitled' to those gilts for time between the sale and resale for the purpose of certain tax relieving provisions for 'entitled' gilts holders ('no': *IRC v Scottish Provident Institution* [2005] STC 15); and whether options issued and exercised to yield no economic profit or loss (because of how these options were priced) nevertheless produced a 'loss' for the purposes of TCGA 1992, section 16 ('no': *Schofield v HMRC* [2012] STC 2019).

Importantly, this provision-by-provision approach did not rely on a notion of 'tax avoidance' as a term of art, either in isolation or in contradistinction to 'tax mitigation'. Despite the distinction between the two terms in *IRC v Willoughby* [1997] STC 995, the case law in this area asked a different question: 'did the transaction under scrutiny meet the criteria demanded in the relevant statute to achieve the result sought by the taxpayer?' This was in the light of the facts, the 'relevance' of which was determined by reference to that same statute.

(2) *UBS: a watershed.* The cases discussed so far disclosed a hostility to tax avoidance on a provision-by-provision basis. This hostility was elevated to a general norm, free of any specific statutory provision, by the Supreme Court's decision in *UBS.* Prior to *UBS,* the provision-by-provision purposive approach assumed that the specific statutory provision engaged in a particular case applied in a particular way to the specific transaction in that case, such that a tax avoidance motivation was or was not relevant to the application of that provision. So, the financing of an interest obligation by lending the borrower another loan, so that the borrower may pay the outstanding interest to crystallise tax relief on the 'payment' of interest (for the purpose of the Income and Corporation Taxes Act 1988, section 338) succeeded in obtaining tax relief for the payer, even in the face of an accusation that the only reason for the fresh loan was to allow the borrower to obtain the tax relief. This was on the basis that the specific provision was indifferent to any tax-driven motivations and considered 'payment' to mean nothing more than the satisfaction of a legal liability: *Westmoreland Investments Ltd v MacNiven* [2001] STC 237 ('*Westmoreland*').

In *UBS,* it was critical to the success of a tax avoidance scheme that certain securities issued by a company were viewed as the 'provision' of these securities within the meaning of ITEPA 2003, section 423(1). The UK Supreme Court held that because one of the purposes of the legislation in question was to counteract tax avoidance, the word 'provision', applied to 'securities' in the relevant statute ought to be interpreted as 'provision having a business or commercial purpose' (so that there was no 'provision' in this case, as the issue was for tax avoidance purposes alone and the scheme failed: [78], [85], per Lord Reed). This was so even though the relevant section (section 423) was silent about whether this 'provision' was part of tax avoidance arrangements or not, whereas other provisions in the same Act (Income Tax (Earnings and Pensions) Act 2003 (ITEPA 2003)) expressly referred to tax avoidance and excluded their application in tax avoidance arrangements. According to the UK Supreme Court, there was no inference from these latter provisions that Parliament, in enacting section 423, was indifferent to whether the 'provision' of securities was part of a tax avoidance scheme or not. So the fact that the issue of the relevant securities was part of an avoidance scheme, with no 'business or commercial purpose', was sufficient to exclude the application of section 423.

The reading of words into a statutory provision (here 'having a business or commercial purpose' into section 423(1) of ITEPA 2003), even tax provisions, is not novel: see *Inco Europe* and chapter two. What changed in *UBS* was that hostility towards tax avoidance which might be identified as an aspect of the perceived purpose of a particular statutory provision became a recognition that hostility to tax avoidance (and a judicial responsibility to frustrate avoidance) was a strong legal norm of general application.

UBS marks a watershed. As observed above, the silence of section 423 on 'tax avoidance', by contrast with other provisions of Part 7 of ITEPA 2003, which contained section 423, did not, for Lord Reed, give rise to any inference that section 423 was indifferent to whether tax avoidance was the sole driver for the issue of the relevant securities. So statutory context (that is, the inference raised by other provisions in the same statute which did mention 'tax avoidance', suggesting that the silence of section 423 on 'tax avoidance' meant that such tax avoidance was simply irrelevant) yielded to something else. What is this something else? Lord Reed does not specify the basis of the Supreme Court's construction of the term 'provision'. Certainly the reprehensibility of tax avoidance as a norm informed Lord Reed's approach. But was this the application of a social attitude to a value laden statutory term? Not really: the term 'provision' is neither value laden, nor sufficiently elastic to admit the words 'with a business etc purpose'.

The other candidate basis is the technique in *Inco Europe Ltd v First Choice Distributions* [2000] 1 WLR 858 ('*Inco Europe*') of reading words into statutes, discussed in chapter two. If *UBS* were to be properly viewed as an application of *Inco Europe* (Lord Reed does not say this is the case), this would represent the emergence of the reprehensibility of tax avoidance as a Parliamentary objective which, even if although unexpressed, is sufficiently strong, clear and precise to apply (in favour of HMRC) to all statutory provisions and permit these provisions to have words read into them to frustrate the perceived avoidance (subject to Parliament's contrary express or necessarily implied intention).

The strength of this legal norm is apparent from its resistance to the inference which would naturally be drawn from the express reference to tax avoidance in other sections of the Act. Indeed, the approach of the UK Supreme Court in *UBS* assumes that the norm (principle) that tax avoidance is reprehensible (and that words should be read into provisions so as to frustrate tax avoidance) is sufficiently embedded in the law as a matter of general application, and that this norm is clear enough to permit anti-tax avoidance language to be read by implication into *any* statutory provision, irrespective of (1) the absence of any reference to tax avoidance in that provision) and (2) the inferences which may otherwise arise from other provisions in the same Act.

Such an approach also extends the reach of the *Inco Europe* technique. Unless the reprehensibility of tax avoidance as a strong, clear and precise legal norm was present when ITEPA 2003 was enacted, Lord Reed's approach, if it is an application of *Inco Europe*, extends the reading in of words not only to correcting drafting errors at the time of enactment but to circumstances where, at the time of construction, the *current* Parliament would consider the provision under scrutiny to be deficient. Parliament is to be taken (at the time of enactment of all tax statutes) to have an objective of accommodating changes in social attitudes and legal attitudes to tax avoidance and having developed a strong, precise general hostility to tax avoidance by the time of that the avoidance schemes were implemented to permit anti-avoidance language to be read into section 423.

Put another way, the assumption made by Lord Reed that one of Part 7 of ITEPA 2003's objectives is to combat tax avoidance is a recognition of the strong legal norm that tax avoidance is always contrary to the purposes of the tax legislation in question because of a general legislative intent to legislate by reference to real economic activities: Hodge 2017, 9. Lord Hodge's reference to 'real world transactions with real world economic effects' is taken from *Barclays Mercantile Business Finance v Mawson* [2002] EWCA Civ 1853, at [66] (per Carnwath LJ), cited in *UBS* at [64] and thus the only limitation to applying this legal anti-avoidance norm is any linguistic limitation (express or by implication) to be found in the relevant provisions. For example, while a court may read in words to qualify express words, a court cannot, in so doing, distort the express language of a statutory provision.

That there is now a general legal norm, which assumes legislative intent against tax avoidance, is explicit in obiter dicta in *Hurstwood Properties Ltd v Rossendale Borough Council* [2021] UKSC 16. Lord Briggs and Lord Leggatt, in a unanimous UK Supreme Court judgment, say that 'it is not generally to be expected that Parliament intends to exempt from tax a transaction which has no purpose other than tax avoidance' (at [11]). This appeal to express appeal to general legislative intent makes visible what was implicit in *UBS*. The UK Supreme Court

does not directly apply an extra-legal norm that tax avoidance is reprehensible in an illegitimate *Roberts v Hopwood* manner, ignoring statutory
provisions altogether. Even under the general formulation in *Hurstwood*,
the strong general norm that tax avoidance is reprehensible (a presumption in HMRC's favour) is applied through the medium of a permitted
construction of a specific provision. But this approach does put enormous pressure on the courts to identify 'tax avoidance' in the eyes of the
reasonable legislature as a matter of statutory construction, which is not
an easy or precise task.

THE EFFECT OF THE REPREHENSIBILITY OF TAX AVOIDANCE AS AN INDEPENDENT GENERAL LEGAL NORM

There are two important senses in which tax avoidance's reprehensibility is an independent legal norm, and one important sense in which it
is not.

It is an independent legal norm in that (1) it has juridical content
independent of the social attitudes from which it grew, and (2) it can
attach to and inform legal rules other than those specific provisions to
which it is applied i.e., it is capable of 'floating'. In a third sense, it is *not*
independent; its invocation is not sufficient of itself to dispose of a claim
to tax by a taxing authority. This is true of many legal norms, as distinguished from legal rules.

There is a conceptual limitation on the effect (through interpretation) of this strong general legal norm. This strong general legal norm
cannot have direct substantive effect as a specific rule of tax law. It is a
presumptive principle only. So cases such as *Westmoreland* remain good
law (certainly *UBS* did not suggest the contrary). Transactions undertaken purely for tax purposes may be respected even in tax statutes if
the relevant provision, construed even in the light of this strong general
legal norm, is properly applied to confer the result sought by a taxpayer.
Ironically, this strong general legal norm requires the courts to scrutinise specific tax provisions more carefully than ever to see whether they
exclude its application.

Where does the legitimacy of (1) accommodating anti-tax avoidance
sentiments and (2) this strong new general legal norm come from? And
what gives the norm its specific content? The answer to both questions

is a combination of social attitudes and the current legal norms which reflect those attitudes.

First, the concepts to which the norm that 'tax avoidance is reprehensible' have hitherto attached are value-laden or ambulatory concepts, for example, 'unconscionability' and 'legislative purpose', or 'reasonableness', all of which can admit social attitudes (as discussed above).

Second, the transmogrification of anti-tax avoidance into a general legal norm of considerable strength finds legitimate legal roots in the background legal regime, which has changed radically over the last decade. Parliament has expressed hostility to tax avoidance at a general level, not merely in the context of specific taxes and specific transactions, for example, in so-called targeted anti-avoidance provisions, 'TAARs', examples of which include TCGA 1992, section 16A (capital losses disallowed in arising from avoidance schemes) and CTA 2009, section 441 (corporate debt transactions with a 'main' tax avoidance purpose denied tax relief for finance costs and losses).

Examples of Parliament's general distaste for tax avoidance are to be found in Parliament's introduction of legislation requiring the disclosure of tax avoidance schemes (Finance Act 2004, Part 7), deterring the activities of 'promoters' (Finance Act 2014, Part 5, Schedules 33A to 36) and 'enablers' (Finance (No 2) Act 2017, Schedule 16) of tax avoidance schemes, and the General Anti-Abuse Rule ('GAAR'), which negates tax advantages that would otherwise accrue to those who enter into schemes that are 'abusive', that is, which cannot reasonably be regarded as a reasonable course of action in relation to the relevant tax provisions (Finance Act 2013, section 207(2); and see Part 5 more generally).

The legal antipathy, especially as illustrated by the GAAR, to tax avoidance is overwhelming and obvious. This legal backdrop extends to a supra-national anti-tax avoidance attitude: the OECD has concluded that (tax) base erosion and profit shifting (BEPS) is worthy of sustained and focussed attention: see OECD 2015. The courts and the legislature are iteratively each giving the other momentum to develop anti-tax avoidance attitudes (which carries the responsibility to identify in each case what is 'avoidance'). Thus, the elevation of 'tax avoidance is reprehensible' to a general (strong) legal norm is legitimate, both by reference to social attitudes for value laden concepts and to the current legislative background which clearly deplores tax avoidance. A perfectly apt analogue is the framework of equalities legislation, which now has a highly visible commitment to equality (and protection from discrimination) on grounds of race, gender and so on. There is a strong legal norm (equality of treatment on these grounds) which will inform the construction of all statutes.

However, it must be remembered that this new general norm of construction applies if (and only if) avoidance is found to inform the relevant transaction. And as observed above, the identification of 'avoidance' (by contrast to 'mitigation') is an imprecise exercise, certainly if the avoidance/mitigation distinction is to be resurrected. So although a general anti-tax avoidance anti-avoidance attitude is easy to sympathise with (especially in the light of the current background statutory regime), it must also be recognised that predictability and consistency are undermined to the extent that the trigger condition for this new general norm (a finding of 'avoidance') is itself uncertain and imprecise.

SUMMARY

The key idea that tax avoidance is reprehensible is a legal norm may be summarised as follows:

(1) Tax avoidance is defined as the reduction of one's tax liabilities (whether escaping or deferring a tax charge on otherwise taxable amounts or obtaining deductions without incurring any burden) without the invitation of Parliament. To the extent that such an invitation is shown to exist on a purposive interpretation of the statute in context, the reduction in liability is tax mitigation. Tax avoidance is reprehensible; tax mitigation is not. Whether there is 'avoidance' is a critical anterior question which the courts must answer before applying any anti-avoidance presumption. This is a very difficult exercise to undertake with any consistency. An example is the decision of the House of Lords in *Westmoreland*: to borrow to repay a loan was not 'avoidance' in the context of the particular provision and so there was no scope for the application of any presumptive anti-avoidance norm, new notions of 'avoidance' (and new uncertainties) may well emerge (indeed it is not clear whether all of the anti-avoidance sentiments referred to above have the same notion of 'avoidance' in mind).

(2) 'Tax avoidance is reprehensible' has evolved from a social norm into a strong general legal norm. Whereas social norms cannot of themselves apply as legal norms, they can be transformed into legal

norms if an 'access condition' tied to the legal framework in question is satisfied.

(3) That evolution has been made possible by the mediating effect of other legal machinery, most notably equitable jurisdictions which adopt and apply value laden notions (*Bhaur*) and techniques of construction (*Ramsay*).

(4) Through this process, the proposition that 'tax avoidance is reprehensible' has developed its own juridical content as a strong general legal norm. This is the first sense in which 'tax avoidance is reprehensible' is an *independent* legal norm: its content is not necessarily tied to the content of the corresponding social norm out of which it grew.

(5) The second sense in which it is independent is that the content and application of this strong general legal norm is separate from the content of any specific tax provision.

(6) The proposition that 'tax avoidance is reprehensible' is not, without more, a ground for the determination of a legal dispute. Because it is a legal norm (ie, a principle or a standard) rather than a rule in itself, its effect is necessarily mediated by specific rules.

RESPONSES TO CHAPTER FIVE

JONATHAN PEACOCK KC, 11 NEW SQUARE

The notion that 'tax avoidance is bad' is both a social norm and now a legal norm which, in an appropriate statutory context, can found a conclusion as to the interpretation of a particular provision of a tax code is an important one. And as this chapter makes clear, it is an approach, even perhaps a 'principle', which is well-grounded in the authorities. Three observations might usefully be made, one trite (but neverthe-less important), the second of greater nuance and the third designed to provoke a wider debate.

First, the difficulty of drawing a sharp distinction between tax 'miti-gation and tax 'avoidance' cannot be underestimated. While the classic golf club bore might talk in terms of 'planning' his affairs or 'mitigation' of his liabilities, the relevant Revenue officer might reasonably consider the steps in question to be 'avoidance'. Even drawing a line by reference to what Parliament must have intended leaves the casual observer grasp-ing at smoke: buying an investment inside a 'tax-free' wrapper like an Individual Savings Account (ISA) would not commonly be seen as 'avoid-ance' but buying the same investment inside an over-funded personal pension might be. It is all a question of perception, of fact, of the particu-lar statutory intention. Such questions are ones the courts continue to struggle to answer in a consistent, principled way.

Second, the authorities discussed above make clear that it is an approach to 'artificial tax avoidance' (per Lord Walker in *Pitt v Holt*) that attracts the status of both social and legal norm. But that simply begs a different question, namely what it is that determines the pres-ence, as a sub-set of 'avoidance' generally, of 'artificial' avoidance? Much the same question arises in relation to the phrase commonly used by politicians – such and such an activity amounts to 'aggressive' or 'abusive' tax avoidance. There is, as yet, no proper legal answer to this exercise in taxonomy, although interestingly the House of Commons Library proceeds on the basis that:

> Tax avoidance is to be distinguished from tax evasion, where someone acts against the law. By contrast tax avoidance is compliant with the law, though

aggressive or abusive avoidance, as opposed to simple tax planning, will seek to comply with the letter of the law, but to subvert its purpose. (Tax Avoidance and Tax Evasion, 24 Nov 2021)

With respect, this is not good enough; it is not enough to permit 'simple tax planning' and treat all other behaviours as 'aggressive or abusive' when the courts appear, at the moment, to draw a different, subtler, distinction. Standing back, while the relevant classification of activities remains to be explored in future cases, students, jurists and practitioners need to be alive to the need for precision in both language and concept when addressing the developing legal norm.

Third, and as this chapter recognises, the difficulty of grounding the 'tax avoidance is bad' norm and of justifying its use in a given case means that the application of such an approach is necessarily uncertain. This means, in turn, that the predictability of the UK tax code and the consistency of its application are undermined, possibly to a significant extent. In a world where capital and (to a lesser degree) people move freely, and the UK is (post-Brexit) competing for economic activity and growth, one wonders whether the uncertainty which may result from the application of imprecise judge-made (or at least judge-recognised) principles of anti-avoidance may cause more damage overall to the UK than the very 'avoidance' being challenged. And this is all the more so when Parliament and the Tax Authorities have other, more precise, statutory remedies in the form of TAARs and the GAAR.

Author's response: Mr Peacock calls out the inherent difficulty of identifying the reprehensible 'tax avoidance' which is the target of the social and legal norms discussed in this chapter. And Mr Peacock is clearly right in suggesting that 'artificiality' is a good touchstone (is a transaction or step explained only by its tax-driven objective? Is this what is legitimately attacked by an anti-avoidance principle?). And the observation made in this chapter that that the social attitude of what is 'tax avoidance' is not obviously a common, homogeneous idea makes clear the importance of the courts telling us what they mean by 'avoidance' and also attracts the debate as to whether the uncertainty created by notions of 'tax avoidance' may sometimes outweigh the good done by attacking 'tax avoidance' in some generic sense.

DAVID EWART KC, PUMP COURT TAX CHAMBERS

I have spent a great (perhaps too great!) part of my professional life litigating tax avoidance schemes on both sides of the fence. In many of these cases, the judges have approached the matter neutrally and treated it as an intellectual exercise in applying the case law to the facts. 'Hostility' has been restricted to highly artificial transactions which bear no relation to commercial (or sometimes legal) reality. By contrast, some schemes involve ordinary commercial transactions and have enduring consequences. *Furniss v Dawson* is an example of this. The taxpayer succeeded before the Special Commissioner, Vinelott J and the Court of Appeal. Even in the House of Lords, Lord Brightman began his leading speech:

> 'My Lords, the transaction which we are called upon to consider is not a tax avoidance scheme, but a tax deferment scheme ... The scheme before your Lordships is a simple and honest scheme which merely seeks to defer payment of tax until the taxpayer has received into his hands the gain which he has made.'

This vividly illustrates Jonathan Peacock's point that it is sometimes difficult to distinguish between tax avoidance and tax mitigation. It may also suggest that the distinction is not very important unless one is considering a provision which specifically refers to tax avoidance.

Despite these difficulties, Julian Ghosh is right to say that tax avoidance is generally regarded as reprehensible. It might, however, be helpful to ask why that is the case. Or, more importantly, why it ought to be the case.

The reprehensible element in tax avoidance is really a matter of basic fairness and civic duty ('not an exercise is good citizenship'). It is regarded as wrong that, in some circumstances, individuals or companies should obtain an advantage over other taxpayers. Obviously, there will always be some who are more able or better advised than others and so will inevitably obtain advantages. What are the circumstances in which that advantage should be regarded as illegitimate? There is no obvious touchstone for answering that question. The instinctive reaction is that it is unfair if a person's liability to tax depends upon transactions which have an air of 'Alice in Wonderland'. Typically, this might include a very large 'payment' for an entirely uncommercial quid pro quo which passes in a circle by way of a series of self-cancelling transactions which usually are carried out by way of book entries. It is these types of features, rather than the minimisation of tax in itself, which is regarded as deserving censure.

Finally, a word or two about *UBS*. I do not see it as so much of a watershed. It seems to me to be part of the logical, incremental development of the law in this area. It builds upon the decision of Lord Hoffmann in *Carreras Group v Stamp Commission* [2004] STC 1377 and the vivid remarks of Carnwath LJ in *Barclays Mercantile v Mawson* [2003] STC 66 at paragraph [66]:

> It recognises the underlying characteristic of all taxing statutes, as parasitic in nature. They draw their life-blood from real world transactions with real world economic effects, to which the Revenue is not a party. To allow tax treatment to be governed by transactions which have no real world purpose of any kind is inconsistent with that fundamental characteristic.

In fact in *UBS*, Lord Reed did not base his decision on any broad principle of universal application to taxing statutes. Far from it, he carried out a detailed analysis of the provisions under consideration in paragraphs [73]–[84] before coming to his purposive construction at paragraph [85]. I find it difficult, in that careful and detailed analysis, to detect any moral censure. I have never read *UBS* as introducing the idea that tax avoidance is reprehensible. This perhaps demonstrates that the same text can yield different fruit for different readers.

Author's response: The consensus on both tax avoidance's reprehensibility as orthodoxy and the difficulty of distinguishing avoidance and mitigation amongst the respondents and the author is telling. However, I disagree that the avoidance-mitigation distinction is relevant only or mainly to provisions specifically dealing with 'avoidance' on their face. Bhaur was a case on a discretionary remedy and the approach of the Court of Appeal turns on whether there was a 'social evil' or not. Our disagreement on UBS is about legal technique. Lord Reed makes a statutory assumption that transactions with no commercial purpose ought not to achieve their desired tax effect (statutory rather than moral reprehensibility if you like but this attitude must come from somewhere). And the meaning of the term 'provision' must depend on a particular legal technique (linguistic construction or reading in words) and the robust application of one or other of these is what is new in UBS. Readers (along with the judges of the Court of Appeal, whose unanimous decision was reversed by the UK Supreme Court) are invited to consider whether UBS *is indeed an unsurprising incremental addition to avoidance case law or something more radical.*

MALCOLM GAMMIE KC, ONE ESSEX COURT

The author of this short volume demonstrates his mastery of the subject on every page. In doing so he provides an excellent introductory insight into the world of tax law, designed to provoke debate and challenge thinking on the subject.

Tax, it has been suggested, is what we pay for civilised society: *Compania General de Tabacos de Filipinas v Collector of Internal Revenue* (1927) 275 US 87, at 100 (per Justice Oliver Wendell Holmes). Civilised societies adhere to the rule of law and law provides the rules that society imposes on its members to regulate their conduct. If rules are imposed in an area in which there is no universal moral imperative to aid understanding, they should usually aim to be clear and unequivocal: Oliver 1993, 173.

The Corleone family presumably called upon certain residents of New York to contribute to the society in which they lived. No doubt the family's demand was clear and unequivocal. But was that tax, or a payment for the family's protection? Certainly, it was not the law of a civilised society.

Civilised societies legislate for tax but, in doing so, frequently struggle to provide clarity, leaving taxpayers (and their legal advisers) uncertain as to the tax they must pay. Why is that so and should we tolerate it?

If you want to cross the River Thames, you can pass free through the Blackwall Tunnel or pay a toll at the Dartford Crossing. The toll (and the circumstances in which it must be paid) are clear and unequivocal. Is that a tax or a user fee? If a tax, do you avoid tax at the Crossing if you choose the Tunnel? Does the answer to the previous question depend upon the reason you give for your choice of the Tunnel?

What was clear and unequivocal initially is no longer so in the presence of a rule aimed at toll avoiders. And if a person who uses the Tunnel to avoid the toll gives false reasons for doing so, what was 'avoidance' becomes 'evasion'.

This simple example illustrates that clarity in taxation depends upon the ease with which the elements of the charge can be defined in legislation. The scope for tax avoidance depends upon what is sought to be taxed (the tax base) and the ease with which what is taxed can be substituted by something else. When is substitution good and when is it bad? By comparison, tax evasion depends upon the ability of the Revenue authority to effectively check and enforce liability.

All these elements of taxation reflect legislative choices made by Governments and Parliaments. Some would say that if you cannot adequately describe in legislation the subject matter of taxation, then you should not seek to tax it. The authors of the Memorandum of Dissent to the Final Report of the 1955 Royal Commission on *The Taxation of Profits and Income* expressed the view that, 'the existence of widespread tax avoidance is evidence that the system, not the taxpayer, stands in need of radical reform': Woodcock, Bullock and Kaldor 1955. Pending reform, however, lawyers and the courts will continue to struggle with the legal problems of taxation and avoidance that the author outlines.

Author's response: Malcolm Gammie KC is one of the most distinguished tax lawyers in the UK of the last 50 years. So his complaint that a lack of analytical clarity in tax provisions of itself is a driver for so-called avoidance must be taken seriously. Mr Gammie's response shows the inter-connection of each and every chapter in this book: 'tax' and its component parts must be defined before the nature of a 'tax obligation' can be assessed. And 'avoidance' takes its colour from these anterior exercises. But Mr Gammie's response is in truth a challenge to the courts and academics alike to identify the criteria of what makes a 'tax' in order to identify what is (or is not) reprehensible 'avoidance' (again the distinction between avoidance and mitigation and a need to identify what distinguishes them is revealed as vital). Readers are invited to consider Mr Gammie's central thesis (clarity would reduce avoidance) and ask whether this is apparent in the courts' approach (and if not, whether it ought to be).

6

Philosophers Misled

1. INTRODUCTION

The legitimacy of taxation (and of particular tax laws) is an obvious subject for discussion and debate amongst political philosophers. Key ideas *within* tax are open to normative interrogation. Why should a particular class of persons be exempted from being a 'taxable person' altogether? Why should certain receipts be excluded from the tax base of one or more taxable persons? Why should the tax base be increased by deeming provisions which impute market value? This is even more obviously so in relation to key ideas *about* tax: why should tax be fixed on a class of taxable persons at all? Indeed, is tax ever legitimate or is it only legitimate to achieve certain objectives only? So it might be argued that tax is legitimate to finance public goods (howsoever defined) but nothing else. And is tax a legitimate mode to deliver a particular objective (say redistribution) or is another mode more legitimate (say compulsory purchase and redistribution of property, especially as tax imposes a money obligation, not a property obligation)?

These debates, insofar as they scrutinise *tax law*, should have the legal characteristics of tax law in mind. The preceding chapters of this book have sought to make those characteristics clear: in particular that, so far as taxes in the UK are concerned (and most taxes imposed in other jurisdictions throughout the world) juristically, a tax is a personal money obligation, not a property obligation, which operates as a mode and may fulfil various functions. It is possible to have a debate about whether the imposition of an obligation to deliver monies (however the quantum of the obligation is calculated) is ever legitimate (whatever mode tax operates in or objective it seeks to fulfil). It is equally possible to have a debate about whether this money obligation is appropriate to fulfil certain objectives, such as the finance of public goods, but not others, such as redistribution, either because the mode of taxation is legitimate/ illegitimate or because the objective is legitimate/illegitimate. In the latter case, however, the debate is not about tax law as such at all but rather the legitimacy of the objective.

The key complaint in this chapter is that philosophers who engage in such debates generally do not define 'taxation' at all, let alone differentiate amongst different types of taxes. Some philosophers debate the legitimacy of taxation without mentioning what they mean by 'taxation' (which means that any debate is an air shot), or on mistaken assumptions about taxation (in particular on the assumption that taxation imposes a property obligation, not a personal monetary obligation). In particular, these latter debates not only miss the point (there is no point is attacking or defending taxation on the basis that it should or should not attack property rights if taxation does not attack property rights at all.

To be sure, if and to the extent that taxation did impose a proprietary obligation, any attack or defence of taxation must scrutinise the relationship and legitimacy of property rights and taxation's qualification of these. Where there is no proprietary obligation, where taxation is not a compulsory purchase, any attack or defence of taxation by reference to property rights is wrong in principle. The comments made below are restricted to cases where taxes are non-proprietorial money debts. But to be clear, the Internal Revenue Code 1954, section 6151 (the predecessor of 26 USC 6313, which also made clear that a United States tax obligation was non-proprietary) was in force in the United States at the time at which Nozick wrote *Anarchy, State and Utopia* (Nozick 1974) and USC 6313 was in force at the time at which Murphy and Nagel wrote the *Myth of Ownership* (Murphy and Nagel 2002). So the personal, non-proprietary nature of a tax obligation in the United States was clear at the time that these American writers, whose debate is discussed below, considered the nature of tax law.

An illustration is the debate arising out of Robert Nozick's attack on the legitimacy of taxation (made at a time when taxes in the United States were certainly non-proprietorial money debts). Nozick's criticism of taxation rested on the basis that to attack property rights is to attack the personhood of the property owner, viewed through the lens of self-ownership. The response offered by Liam Murphy and Thomas Nagel in defence of taxation is that there are no property rights in anything, including pre-tax income, unless and until legitimate demands over those things, including tax liabilities, have been discharged.

Both sides of the debate provide highly visible examples of philosophical analysis in which the positions of each party to the debate would have had greater focus and clarity had these been founded on a precise and correct appreciation of the legal nature of taxation, without the distraction of looking at property rights. In that sense, the Nozick–Murphy and Nagel debate shows how each of the errors indicated above can reinforce the other: the argument proceeds on a mistaken assumption about taxation (by supposing that it is properly understood as standing in contradistinction to property rights) precisely because it does not consider the legal nature of taxation at all.

The remainder of this chapter analyses both sides of this argument, drawing out the structural deficiencies resulting from these misunderstandings of the nature of taxation.

2. MISCONCEIVED LIBERTARIAN HOSTILITY

For Nozick, taxation is a qualification of property rights and thus an attack on self-ownership: 'individuals have rights, and there are things which no individual or group can do to them (without violating these rights)': Nozick 1974, ix. This protection of rights arises from 'the Kantian principle that individuals are ends not merely means; they may not be sacrificed or used for the achieving of other ends without their consent' (30–31). This principle of moral equality confers dignity upon each person and 'allows [persons] … to choose [their] life and realize [their] ends and [their] conception of [themselves] … aided by the voluntary cooperation of other individuals possessing the same dignity' (334).

Nozick regards property rights as comprised in 'an entitlement theory', whereby if it is assumed that everyone is entitled to the goods they currently possess (their 'holdings'), a just distribution of property rights arises as a result purely from people's free exchanges. A just entitlement is a function of the application of three principles (160): the principle of transfer (whatever is justly acquired may be freely transferred); the principle of just initial acquisition of things which may then be transferred; and the principle of rectification of injustice (how to deal with holdings unjustly acquired or transferred). (See Kymlicka 2002, 103–04 for a penetrating summary of Nozick's entitlement theory.)

Central to Nozick's view of property rights is a claim to self-ownership, which is violated by any demand that goods produced by the talented be used to improve the well-being of the disadvantaged. Such demands 'institute (partial) ownership by others of people and their labour. These principles involve a shift from the classical liberals' idea of self-ownership to a notion of (partial) property-rights in other people' (Nozick 1974, 172). Thus any demands upon a person's labour or its fruits is an attack on self-ownership (171, 172).

Famously, Nozick's logic is that tax reduces the fruits of one's labour, so 'taxation of earnings from labour is on a par with forced labour' (169). People have property in themselves and their labour, which entails the right to decide what work to do. Accordingly, seizing the results of someone's labour is 'equivalent to seizing hours from him and directing him to carry on various activities'. This process of the state removing the ability of persons to decide what work to do and what to do with its proceeds 'gives [the state] a property right' in the persons so compelled. In this, Nozick follows Locke 1689: 'every Man has a Property in his own person ... The labour of his Body, and the Work of his Hands, we may say, are properly his' (paragraph 27, cited in 'A Discourse on Property: John Locke and his Adversaries' Mervyn S Johnson July 1982, Wiley online library), a proposition which informs the further Lockean observation that 'if any one shall claim a Power to lay and levy Taxes on the People by his own authority, and without the consent of the people, he thereby invades the Fundamental Law of Property ... For what property have I in that which another may by right take when he pleases himself?' (paragraph 140; discussed in Snape and Hughes 2017). Modern libertarians echo the notion of tax as an appropriation of property: for example, Oakeshott regards tax as a transfer of property to the ruler, not merely a constraint on action, which can be legitimised only by 'consent' (Oakeshott 1999, 178).

On Nozick's argument, if forced labour to serve the needy is illegitimate, then the seizure of people's goods by means of taxation for that same purpose cannot be legitimate (Nozick 1974, 172). Thus only a minimal state, 'limited to the narrow functions of protection against force, theft, fraud, and enforcement of contracts and so on' is legitimate (at 172). Any financing of additional state activities involves the coercive taxation of people, violating the principle 'from each as they choose, to each as they are chosen' (at 172).

Nozick deploys a 'one-step' argument: taxation is illegitimate *simply because* it expropriates the taxpayer's property (and is thus an attack on his self-ownership). But as observed above, taxation does not expropriate or otherwise qualify the taxpayer's property rights in any of his property. None of his identifiable assets are subject to a tax claim. None of the 'fruits' of a taxpayer's labours (pre-tax profits) are the *subject* of a tax claim, only money, wherever the taxpayer may find it (including inherited funds or a gift from another – the 'fruits' of someone else's labours). This is true whether or not one accepts Nozick's notion of self-ownership as regards property rights. So Nozick's hostility to taxation cannot legitimately be predicated on a notion of taxation as a claim to a taxpayer's property.

Of course, Nozick might well say that even if, contrary to his thesis, taxation does not, as a matter of juristic analysis, expropriate a taxpayer's property, taxation (beyond the financing of public goods) treats people as means, not ends, by compelling them to participate in the projects of others (redistribution of wealth and other egalitarian objectives). On that view, juristic distinctions between claims to money and claims against property are irrelevant. But even then Nozick would have to confront the specific nature of taxation and the various bases on which tax may be imposed to demonstrate that one or more of them offended Kantian moral equality and his notion of self-ownership.

Laying aside any redistributive objective of taxation, taxation as, say, a tool of social engineering may increase the efficiency of the marketplace and be closer to the provision of public goods than Nozick might realise. Or taxation as a tool of economic management may increase market efficiency (or ensure its survival). The structural flaw in Nozick's analysis is therefore twofold. First, a recognition that taxation is a claim to money, not to property, would force Nozick to justify his hostility to one or more of taxation's individuated specific features, objectives or bases. Second, conceptualising taxation simply as an incursion on property rights disregards the modality that (as argued in chapter two) is central to the juristic nature of taxation.

3. MISCONCEIVED EGALITARIAN DEFENCE

The analysis above demonstrates that an egalitarian need not deny a taxpayer's property rights in their pre-tax profits to defend taxation.

The proper method of assessing the justice of a legitimising egalitarian basis of taxation or any other feature of taxation against a libertarian argument (including those based on self-ownership) is to scrutinise taxation's objectives and consequences and subject those objectives and consequences to a normative assessment. There is no need to refer to the taxpayer's property rights.

However, Murphy and Nagel seek to combat libertarian arguments for a minimalist state and hostility to redistributive taxation by meeting the libertarian on his own ground of taxation-as-an-attack-on property-rights (again made at a time when taxes in the United States were non-proprietorial money debts). Thus Murphy and Nagel deny any *property* claims of a taxpayer in his pre-tax profits: 'Taxes must be evaluated as part of the overall system of property rights that they help to create ... the target of evaluation must be the system of property rights that they make possible' (Murphy and Nagel 2002, 8). Taxes must be evaluated as both legal demands by the state on individuals, and as contributions to the framework within which individuals live (42).

Since private property is a legal convention, partly defined by the tax system, the tax system cannot be evaluated by considering its impact on private property as an independent system (8). Markets depend on and are shaped by the decisions of government (which is in turn dependent on taxes). It is therefore, they say, 'logically impossible' that people have any kind of entitlement to their pre-tax income. All they can be entitled to 'is what they would be left with after taxes under a legitimate system, supported by legitimate taxation' (32, 33). As a result, the 'logical order of priority within taxes and property rights is the reverse of that assumed by libertarianism'. Taxes are 'essentially modifications of property rights that entitle the State to control over part of the resources generated by the economic life of its citizens' (44). Thus 'Property rights are not the starting point of [a discussion about taxes] but its conclusion' (10).

In summary, Murphy and Nagel say:

(1) Private property (and indeed government, banks etc) is made possible by taxation.

(2) Without taxation there would be no private property (or any income or wealth).

(3) *Therefore* (to use their precise language) it is logically impossible that people should have any kind of entitlement to their pre-tax income.

(4)   All that anyone is entitled to is what they would be left with after legitimate taxes.

(5)   Thus taxes are 'essentially modifications of property rights that entitle the State to control over [pre-tax profits]'.

Several criticisms may be made of this analysis.

As to (1) and (2), it is obvious that taxation is not *solely* responsible for the creation and protection of private property. Taxation cannot therefore have any sort of exclusive claim to defining property rights.

As to (3), Murphy and Nagel commit a 'naturalistic fallacy', seeking to derive an 'ought' from an 'is' by adopting a 'but for' test. In particular, an 'is' in step (2) – a factual claim about the necessary preconditions of private property – is said to entail an 'ought' in step (3), namely, the conclusion that an 'entitlement' (an evaluative concept) to one's pre-tax income is logically impossible. The latter does not follow from the former: 'while taxation and the redistribution of wealth may ... depend upon the institution of property, the existence of property does not entail any kind of taxation regime or any particular distribution (or maldistribution) of wealth' (Penner 1997, 36–37).

The most fundamental criticism is made by Penner, who observes that Murphy and Nagel make the notion of taxation unintelligible by refusing to acknowledge a prior notion of property rights in pre-tax profits. By contending that *taxation* (ignoring other mechanisms, such as criminal law) cures all injustice in relation to *property* rights in pre-tax profits, Murphy and Nagel 'stray from a discussion of taxation completely' (Penner 2005, 80). If tax 'were just part of that milieu of benefits and burdens which go back and forth', the law of taxation is indistinguishable from, say, criminal law or the law of tort, which undo unjust transactions. In other words, Murphy and Nagel's analysis of taxation eliminates the very concept and distinct characteristics of tax (Penner 2005, 90).

Indeed, Murphy and Nagel seemingly accept this criticism in themselves criticising Blum and Kalven (Blum and Kalven 1952). Blum and Kalven acknowledge the narrowness of evaluating the justice of taxes by reference to traditional tax equity standards but observe that any discussion of the general problem of inequality in relation to the justice of progressive taxes means that 'we discover that we have lost our topic'. Murphy and Nagel's riposte is that 'what [their] observation shows, of course, is that they were discussing the wrong topic' (see Murphy and

Nagel 2002, 132). Why Blum and Kalven can be accused of discussing the wrong topic is nowhere explained by Murphy and Nagel. In fact, it is Murphy and Nagel who are discussing the wrong topic (property law, rather than taxation; and property obligations, rather than obligations to pay money debts).

Penner's criticism here echoes the point made above, that different juristic concepts (contract, property, taxation) perform different (perhaps overlapping but nevertheless distinct) roles. To treat taxation as defining property rights is to fail to individuate taxation as a particular distributive justice mechanism, without distinguishing its role from that of other juristic mechanisms which are themselves tools of distributive justice.

The criticism of Murphy and Nagel in this chapter goes beyond those of Penner. Murphy and Nagel mount a 'one-step' defence of redistributive taxation by arguing for taxation as a notion that qualifies property rights which leads to the same problem as Nozick's 'one-step' attack on taxation. A discussion of the existence of a taxpayer's property rights avoids scrutiny of the nature and legitimising bases of taxation. The debate on a connection between taxation and property rights simply identifies particular ends of distributive (and perhaps corrective) justice, assumes that just property rights should accord with those ends, and defines the scope of taxation to ensure that such property rights are correspondingly wide or narrow (so that taxation is as narrow or wide) to accord with those ends. But a debate on the justice of taxation is a debate as to means, not ends.

In particular, it is a debate as to means which operate at a particular stage of commercial relations. As discussed above, taxation has to be placed alongside other means of distributive (or corrective) justice. Philosophers should respect the range of different juristic notions and their distinctive roles in order to engage in meaningful debate as to their justice. Contract law, employment law and tax law may all have the same objective (protection of vulnerable workers). But common law and statutory mechanisms (including those specific to employment law) which regulate contracts concern whether there is a contract (or a particular term) at all, or whether it is void. Taxation (say a surcharge on employers who pay vulnerable workers a low wage, which is part of a taxable amount contrary to the penalty discussed by the US Supreme Court in *Bailey*) assumes there to be a lawful contract. These different mechanisms impose different rules and merit distinct analyses. Taxation does not seek to qualify property rights of taxable persons and should not be confused with property law.

Once consideration of the justice of taxation is adjusted to respect the distinction between money claims and property claims, philosophers might then serve their own cases better by transferring scrutiny from whether taxation is an interference with property rights to whether taxation on one or more bases is justified. For example, questions as to whether taxation is only legitimate in a democracy may yield a different answer depending on whether taxation is financing public goods or advancing a particular position of distributive or corrective justice. Analysis of whether taxation does (or ought to) affect property rights is simply irrelevant as it simply shifts attention away from taxation towards property rights without addressing the legitimacy of a particular tax charge at all.

Murphy and Nagel are not alone amongst philosophers in trying to combat the self-ownership objections to taxation on Nozick's own terms by seeking to accommodate a claim to legitimate taxation within a notion of just property rights. The issue of taxation has been described by Geoffrey Brennan as the interaction of 'just private property rights and democratically made collective decisions [including a decision to tax which] have independent normative force', albeit that there is no presumption that the 'private property rights structure is to be lexically ordered above democratic decision-making' (Brennan 2018, 63–64). As observed throughout this book (and particularly in chapter three), this observation is incorrect. The issue of taxation is (in any normative assessment) the legitimacy of a claim upon a taxable person to lawfully find money (from anyone or anywhere) and deliver this money to the claimant.

It has also been suggested that 'full legal ownership of a thing precludes the legal permissibility of taxation of the use of the thing or the possession or exercise of those rights' (Vallentyne 2015, 294; see also Vallentyne 2018, which seeks to accommodate taxation in at least certain forms of libertarianism by a precise formulation of property rights). Vallentyne's analysis is echoed by Laura Biron (Biron 2018). Biron observes, correctly, that taxation is a claim for money and distinct from expropriation of property (83, 84) but goes on to assume that taxation and expropriation in fact overlap, in that both may be legitimised by compensation for a taking (84, 85) and both 'limit private property in the name of public interest' (86).

Biron's answer to the question of when taxation is legitimate adopts an analysis very close to that of Vallentyne. She views ownership (89–92) as 'full blooded' but subject to possible qualification (by contrast to 'total ownership' which can never be qualified), so that property ownership consists of a 'bundle' of rights, the scope of which may not be sufficient to resist a tax claim. Biron (91) considers that 'income' is capable of 'ownership' as she views it; it is this 'income' that may be subject to a tax claim that cannot be said to interfere with even 'full blooded' property rights (because those property rights do not, in their scope, protect against legitimate tax claims). Juristic notions are thus effectively ignored and given a 'philosophical' definition on the basis that '[the topic of just taxation] ... is justice, and that is a moral, not a legal, issue' (294).

Vallentyne meets Nozick's complaint against taxation as an attack on rights of self-ownership with the proposition that 'just taxation is compatible with 'almost' full ownership of a thing' (Vallentyne 2015, 295). In other words, the rights of 'full ownership' of a 'thing' (presumably, although Vallentyne does not state as much, money, or, more nebulously, income) is 'weakened to allow expropriation for non-payment of certain taxes' (299) so that self-ownership leads to a right to 'control, use and ... transfer' previously 'unowned resources' but with any 'immunity to losses conditional on the payment of certain taxes' (300). In other words, self-ownership, for Vallentyne, entails the proposition that 'if one fully owns oneself, one stakes a claim to (and/or mixes one's labour with) unowned resources and one compensates anyone who would be disadvantaged by one's appropriation of those resources, then one fully owns those resources, *except that those rights are subject to expropriation if certain taxes are not paid*' (299, emphasis added).

Nozick's notion of 'full self-ownership' is conceded but qualified to accommodate the 'justice of the tax on the transfer of *external* resources (for example money: Nozick 1974, 299) if permitted by a notion of 'justice'. This, for Vallentyne, stems from curing problems of 'market failure', which, in turn, arises from imperfect competition and externalities, where costs or benefits are imposed on individuals without consent, for example, pollution, and 'non-excludable goods' (this being Vallentyne's term for the 'public goods' discussed in chapter one of this work), with an appeal also to paternalistic taxation and redistributive taxation.

Apart from the unhelpful side-stepping of juristic concepts of property and taxation, Vallentyne's recognition that taxation entails the transfer of 'external resources' (money), rather than making any claim on the personal qualities of a moral agent, offers a 'moral' solution to a juristic problem which does not exist. Vallentyne's recognition that money is an 'external resource' should have led Vallentyne to recognise that taxation does not impinge on self-ownership at all (even if self-ownership were a valid foundation upon which to conduct a normative assessment of taxation). Instead Vallentyne concedes self-ownership to entail ownership of the fruits of one's labour but qualifies this latter ownership with a contingent exposure to expropriation if this expropriation is (on some unspecified basis) 'just'. Accordingly, Vallentyne, too, both proceeds on mistaken assumptions about taxation and fails to consider its juristic content.

4. CONCLUSION

Philosophers and jurists, whether libertarians or egalitarians, have done any debate as to the legitimacy of taxation a disservice by making a fundamental category error, in treating taxation as a property obligation rather than a purely personal monetary obligation. Not only is a debate that centres on juristic concepts (here 'property' and 'taxation') misconceived if it gives those juristic concepts mistaken meanings and content, it must necessarily fail to reach an intelligible conclusion, since its subject matter is one which is simply different to that which is in play in imposing (here) the liabilities which are being discussed. The philosophers' debate as to the legitimacy of taxation assumes that a claim to tax is a claim on property, rather than a reply to a question as to the legitimacy of a claim which attacks wealth, or patrimony. Unsurprisingly, they deliver a confused response. A lucid debate as to the legitimacy of taxation requires engagement with the modal objectives and consequences of taxation as a juristic means or method.

The juristic criticisms presented in this chapter are by no means an exhaustive critique of the arguments in question. A puzzling feature of this misconception of taxation as a property right under self-ownership or mixed-labour theories is the failure to address the implications of the fact that most items of property reflect the labours of many moral agents, not just the legal owner. For example, then, the monetary assets (reflecting monetary profits) of an entrepreneur from his widget-making business are mixed not only with the labour of the entrepreneur himself (his investment decisions and risk-taking), but also with the labours of the employee widget-makers and of those who constructed the infrastructure through which the widgets are advertised, sold and transported. As a result, the relevant property rights in cash profits are not, on any mixed labour theory, only those of the legal owner of the cash representing those profits at all. And to the extent that the State, as a separate juristic person, has labour mixed into the cash-property, the State has property rights which may, it might be supposed, be monetised by taxation. This is not to suggest that a liability to taxation is indeed somehow a property obligation (it is not) but rather that the debate which assumes that it is has serious flaws even on its own terms.

RESPONSE TO CHAPTER SIX

PROFESSOR JAMES PENNER, NATIONAL UNIVERSITY OF SINGAPORE

This chapter should be required reading for any philosopher who decides to turn his mind to the topic of tax or taxation, or anyone for that matter interested in the nature of taxation and its justification.

Philosophers haven't always clearly distinguished three questions that must be treated apart:

(1) What are the legitimate purposes of the state?

(2) By what means can the state legitimately pursue those purposes?

(3) Are there any reasons for choosing one particular (legitimate) means over others when pursuing any particular (legitimate) purpose?

As Ghosh demonstrates in chapter two, taxation is a *modal* kind, which cannot be identified with any particular purpose or function which it might be used to realise. Thus, if it can be shown that taxation is a legitimate means at all, this provides a (partial) answer to question (2). But showing this does nothing to answer question (1), which is mainly the question philosophers are trying to answer. And as to question (3), Ghosh provides an illuminating discussion in earlier chapters concerning the different means the state may employ (regulating an area of law such as contract, or applying criminal penalties, or imposing taxes) to achieve the same end, for example distributive justice.

Misidentifying taxation as a functional kind leads to treating the question of the nature of taxation as an answer to question (1), along the lines of 'Is taxation (or more generally the state's raising revenue that in any way impinges upon a person's freedom) a legitimate goal or purpose of the state?' But Ghosh, having identified taxation as a modal kind, shows that this question is simply misconceived.

Moreover, as Ghosh has shown in chapter two, what gives rise to a tax charge is *an activity* (broadly conceived to include what might be called 'passive' activities, such as receiving dividends on shares – though one might also characterise the activity in question as the 'active' activity of investing, that is, entering into financial contracts which generate income). This is very important, because we are concerned here with *legally significant* activities, whether activities in furtherance of fulfilling contractual obligations, legal wrongs such as torts or crimes, or property transactions. Thus, the question of what is a legally significant activity, and legally significant in what way, is conceptually *prior* to the question of how one might tax it.

These basic truths wholly undermine the sense of the Nozick–Nagel and Murphy debate, which Ghosh convincingly criticises. They (and so many others) focus upon the legitimacy or otherwise of what they understand to be property rights, but the problem is general (and they sometimes intuitively recognise this, when 'property' seems capaciously to cover, more or less, all private economic activities). It is only because we can conceive of this activity as a 'property transfer', or more particularly as a case of gift, sale, or inheritance, that is as a legal activity in the first place, that a taxing statute could identify it as subject to a tax charge. The same goes for employment income, a capital gain, a corporate profit, an expense and so on.

As these brief remarks show, this chapter is an invaluable starting place for anyone, whether philosopher or not, who wants to understand what taxation is, what it does, and whether it is a justifiable means for the state to employ in pursuing any of its various purposes.

Author's response: Professor Penner's work on property is what inspired this work, so it is a relief that Professor Penner endorses this chapter's approach. The identification of the importance of identifying the legal relevance of an activity (any activity) to in turn identify which area(s) of law that activity engages is key: otherwise we have a sort of legal imperialism where each area of law vies with others to say 'I apply to this activity, irrespective of the incoherence which results from this, because this activity engages the sort of issues, or sort of issues, that I try to fix, even though these are not exactly the issues within the reach of the legal material (statute and case law) of which I am comprised.' This way lies anarchy. The very existence of different areas of law assumes that they occupy distinct areas of personal and commercial life, which in turn necessitates the identification of what are the core features of each of these different areas of law.

AFTERWORD

DAVID GOLDBERG KC, HEAD OF CHAMBERS,
GRAY'S INN TAX CHAMBERS

The author of this work, who has a deep understanding and a great knowledge of tax, has produced an unusual, interesting book, with two interwoven strands: the first strand may be called the theoretical strand, the second may be called the legal strand.

The theoretical strand begins by identifying the components necessary to create a tax: it feeds into perceptions of the nature of tax as modal rather than functional, as imposing personal rather than proprietary obligations, as creating a distinct area of law which helps to distinguish tax from other forms of impost; and it ends by showing that the lessons learnt from it should have an impact on the philosophy of taxation.

Apparently, the idea explored in chapter three – that tax is a personal obligation – is controversial, though it is unclear what about it creates the controversy: it is surely right that the obligation to pay tax is not proprietary.

The legal strand runs all through the book, bringing with it references to authorities not just from the field of tax but also, and usefully, from other fields which might not always be thought of as cognate and is at its strongest in chapter five on tax avoidance.

The disinclination of taxpayers to pay tax and the inclination of revenue authorities to collect it has led to the wastage, for both sides, of an obstinate struggle and the battlefield is littered with the detritus of failed judicial experiments.

When judges decide cases about what may be called tax avoidance, are they just making it up? Or are they applying some principle, written or unwritten? If so, from where does the principle come?

The author's approach to these questions and his answers to them, given in chapter five, are perceptive and will, to many, be the most illuminating part of the book. He says that the purpose of the chapter is 'to place on a sound juristic footing the proposition, relied on in *Bhaur*, that the social attitude that "tax avoidance is reprehensible" has legal effect' and he achieves that purpose.

Whether it is comfortable to find that a social attitude has transmogrified into a general legal norm is another matter. But discovering by reading this book, that that is what has happened, has been exciting, thought-provoking and enjoyable.

ACKNOWLEDGEMENTS

My first acknowledgement, with thanks and appreciation, is to Lady Rose, Justice of the UK Supreme Court, for agreeing to write the Foreword. It is so very welcome when the senior judiciary engages with academic work. It makes it clear that law (even tax law) is the exclusive province of neither the practitioner, nor the academic.

It is a privilege to contribute to the *Key Ideas* series, which has promoted serious, accessible scholarship. Tax law is under-theorised in the field of analytical jurisprudence but not because jurists have neglected tax law in their work. There are great works on tax law. All of the works about to be mentioned are outstanding examples; of course there are others, there is no negative inference by omission. There are works that deliver an exposition of the UK tax code generally (see for example *Simon's Taxes* (Looseleaf) and *DeVoil's Indirect Tax Service*). There are mighty works on the public international law of taxation (Qureshi and Kumar 2019), cross-border taxation (Baker 2015; Reimer and Rust 2015) and the impact of EU law on Member State tax systems (Wattel, Vermeulen and Marres 2018). There are excellent theoretical analyses of the design of tax systems (Thoronyi 1998; Kay and King 1990) and of specific areas of tax law which have stood the test of time (Gammie and Ball 1982, 1986; Goldberg 1979; Crossey and Baldwin 2021). There are marvellous textbooks (for example, Loutzenhiser 2022), for which students, practitioners and courts are all grateful. But this work seeks to do something different to all of these other works.

Analytical jurisprudence may well have become unfashionable (although this *Key Ideas* series helps to resurrect it). There are wonderful works on the analytical framework of many areas of law, such as English property law (Penner 1997), contract law (Burrows 2020), unjust enrichment (Birks 2005) and the Scots law of obligations (Hogg 2006), which explore the theoretical bases of the legal rules which make up these distinct areas of law. This work seeks to make a contribution, ideally to inspire further scholarship of this type, to tax law.

The value of works such as these is not to make converts (contrast appearing in court). It is to generate discussion and to encourage the pursuit of knowledge. I am extremely grateful to the respondents to each chapter for their contributions (I provide a brief author's reaction to each response): David Ewart KC, Malcolm Gammie KC, Professor Ann Mumford of King's College London, Jonathan Peacock KC, Professor James Penner of the National University of Singapore, Sir Jonathan Richards, Judge of the Chancery Division of the High Court of England and Wales, Nicola Shaw KC and James Wolffe KC. And enormous thanks to David Goldberg KC for his Afterword. These individuals are all not only senior Counsel, judges and academics who have found time to contribute to this work. They have also each made a huge contribution to the development of UK tax law in arguing, deciding and writing about UK tax law. Anyone who comes to this book unfamiliar with tax law should know that the development of UK tax law owes a great deal to each of them.

This work derives from a PhD thesis I wrote at Clare Hall, Cambridge. My examiners were Lord Reed, President of the UK Supreme Court and Professor Timothy Endicott, Vinerian Professor of English Law, of All Souls, Oxford. My viva was a privileged opportunity to discuss the issues I address in this book. I am indebted to both, as I am to my supervisor, Professor (now Emeritus) John Bell, of Pembroke College, Cambridge.

And this work has been made so much better by valuable discussions I have had, with a number of brilliant colleagues at the Tax Bar, which led to real developments in my own thinking. All have deservedly stellar reputations and I am very pleased to work with them at the Bar, as well as to discuss matters of academic interest. Malcolm Gammie KC, James Wolffe KC and Laura Ruxandu, Barrister, subjected this work to particularly fierce interrogation, which had the upside of improving it. Sarah Black, Barrister, Ben Blades, Barrister, and Emilia Carslaw, Barrister, also made invaluable contributions. I especially also mention Louis Triggs, Barrister, who read each and every chapter and made a material contribution not only to editing but also to particular lines of thought. I taught Louis as an undergraduate at King's College London. I am pleased that he has embarked on a career in tax at the Bar, in which (like my other, more senior colleagues I have mentioned) I am sure he will excel.

I should make a special acknowledgment of thanks to Kate Whether and to Linda Goss of Hart and to the whole Hart team, who have been so very helpful and generous in discussing the initial idea of the book and bringing it to fruition.

All errors and omissions are mine. References to any statutory provisions and case law (and to academic works, particularly to specific editions of books that are regularly updated) are as of 30 September 2023.

BIBLIOGRAPHY

Aaronson, G (2016) 'The Swing of the Pendulum: Tax Avoidance in Modern Times' *Tax Journal*. Available at <www.taxjournal.com/articles/swing-pendulum-tax-avoidance-modern-times-28092016>.

Adam, S et al (eds) (2011) *Tax by Design* (Oxford University Press).

Albrecht, AR (1952) 'The Taxation of Aliens Under International Law' 29 *British Year Book of International Law* 152.

Allen, CK (1995) *Law in the Making* 7th edn (Harvard University Press).

Bailey, D and Norbury, N (2020) *Bennion, Bailey and Norbury on Statutory Interpretation* 8th edn (Lexis Nexis).

Baker, P (2005) 'Retrospective Tax Legislation and the European Convention on Human Rights' *British Tax Review* 1.

—— (2015) *Double Taxation Conventions* (Sweet & Maxwell).

Barassi, M (2005) 'The Notion of Tax and the Different Types of Taxes' in Peeters et al (eds), *The Concept of Tax* (International Bureau of Fiscal Documentation).

Barker, WB (2005) 'The Relevance of a Concept of Tax' in Peeters et al (eds), *The Concept of Tax* (International Bureau of Fiscal Documentation).

BBC News (2012) 'Tax Avoidance Schemes "Utterly Immoral", Says Hodge' *BBC News Business* (London, 6 December 2012) <www.bbc.com/news/business-20624848>.

Bell, G (1870) *Commentaries on the Law of Scotland and the Principles of Mercantile Jurisprudence* 7th edn (T & T Clark).

Bhandari, M (2017) 'Introduction' in Bhandari (ed), *Philosophical Foundations of Tax Law* (Oxford University Press).

Bird-Pollan, J (2017) 'The Philosophical Foundations of Wealth Transfer Taxation' in Bhandari (ed), *Philosophical Foundations of Tax Law* (Oxford University Press).

Birks, P (2005) *Unjust Enrichment* (Oxford University Press).

Biron, L (2018) 'Taxing or Taking? Property Rhetoric and the Justice of Taxation' in O'Neill and Orr (eds), *Taxation: Philosophical Perspectives* (Oxford University Press).

Blum, W and Kalven, H (1952) 'The Uneasy Case for Progressive Taxation' 19 *University of Chicago Law Review* 417.

Bowler Smith, M and Ostik, H (2011) 'Towards a Classification of the Central London Congestion Charge as a Tax' 4 *British Tax Review* 487.

Brennan, G (2018) 'Taxation, Justice and the Status of Private Rights' in O'Neill and Orr (eds), *Taxation: Philosophical Perspectives* (Oxford University Press).

Burrows, A (2020) *A Restatement of the English Law of Contract* 2nd edn (Oxford University Press).

Cooper, G (1994) 'The Benefit Theory of Taxation' 11 *Australian Tax Forum* 397.

Crossey, D and Baldwin, M (2021) *Taxation of Partnerships and LLPs* (Sweet & Maxwell).

DeVoil's Indirect Tax Service (LexisNexis).

Duff, D (2017) 'Tax Policy and the Virtuous Sovereign: Dworkinian Equality and Redistributive Taxation' in Bhandari (ed), *The Philosophical Foundations of Tax Law* (Oxford University Press).

Dworkin, R (2002) *Sovereign Virtue* (Harvard University Press).

Elliott, M and Thomas, R (2014) *Public Law* 2nd edn (Oxford University Press).

European Commission (2010) *European System of Accounts* (European Commission).

Feinberg, J (1987) *Harm to Others* (Oxford University Press).

—— (2003) 'Not With My Tax Money: The Problem of Justifying Government Subsidies for the Arts' in Feinberg, *Problems at the Roots of Law: Essays in Legal Thought and Political Theory* (Oxford University Press).

Fleischer, MP (2017) 'How is the Opera Like a Soup Kitchen?' in Bhandari (ed), *The Philosophical Foundations of Tax Law* (Oxford University Press).

Fox, D and Ernst, W (2016) (eds) *Money in the Western Legal Tradition: Middle Ages to Breton Woods* (Oxford University Press).

Friedman, M and Heller, W (1969) *Monetary and Fiscal Policy* (WW Norton & Company Inc).

Fuller, L (1964) *The Morality of Law* (Yale University Press).

Gammie, M (1986) *Tax Strategy for Companies* (Longmans).

Gammie, M and Ball, S (1982) *Tax on Company Reorganizations* (Taxation Publishing).

Gardner, J (2014) *Law as a Leap of Faith* (Oxford University Press).

Goldberg, D (1979) *The Law of Partnership Taxation* (Oyez).

Goldsworthy, J (1999) *The Sovereignty of Parliament* (Oxford University Press).

Goode, R (1987) 'Ownership and Obligation in Commercial Transactions' 103 *Law Quarterly Review* 433.

Goode, R and McKendrick, E (2010) *Goode on Commercial Law* 4th edn (Penguin Books).

Griffith, JAH (1993) *Judicial Politics Since 1920: A Chronicle* (Blackwell).

Hamlin, A (2018) 'What Political Philosophy Should Learn from Economics About Taxation' in O'Neill and Orr (eds), *Taxation: Philosophical Perspectives* (Oxford University Press).

Hart, HLA (1961) 'Kelsen Visited' 10 *University of California Los Angeles Law Review* 179.

—— (2008) *Punishment and Responsibility: Essays in the Philosophy of Law* 2nd edn (Oxford University Press).

—— (2012) *The Concept of Law* 3rd edn (Oxford University Press).

HM Treasury Classification Paper (2010) 'Class (2010) 2 Receipts' (PU975b).

—— (2013) 'Class (2013) 2 Receipts' (PU1548).

Hodge, P (2017) 'The *RFC* Case, Tax Avoidance Schemes and Statutory Interpretation: Offside Goals, Yellow Cards and Own Goals' *Edinburgh Tax Network*, 14 December 2017.

Hogg, M (2006) *Obligations: Law and Language* 2nd edn (Avizandum Publishing Ltd).

Hohfeld, WN (1978) *Fundamental Legal Conceptions as Applied in Judicial Reasoning* (Greenwood Press).

Hyman, D (1990) *Public Finance: A Contemporary Application of Theory to Policy* 3rd edn (Cengage Learning).

Innes, AM (1913) 'What Is Money?' *Banking Law Journal* 32.

International Monetary Fund (2008) *The System of National Accounts* (United Nations).

Institute of Fiscal Studies Meade Committee (1978) *The Structure and Reform of Direct Taxation* (Allen & Unwin).

Kay, JA and King, M (1990) *The British Tax System* (Oxford University Press).

Kelsen, H (1967) *Pure Theory of Law* (University of California Press).

King, J (2008) 'Institutional Approaches to Judicial Restraint' 28 *Oxford Journal of Legal Studies* 409.

Knechtle, A (1979) *Basic Problems in International Fiscal Law* (HFL Publishers).

Kumar, A and Qureshi, AH (eds) (1994) *The Public International Law of Taxation: Texts, Cases and Materials* (Kluwer Law International).

Kymlicka, W (2002) *Contemporary Political Philosophy* (Oxford University Press).

Lee, N et al (eds) (2016) *Revenue Law: Principles and Practice* 34th edn (Bloomsbury).

Locke, J (1689) *Second Treatise of Government*.

Loughlin, M (2010) *Foundations of Public Law* (Oxford University Press).

Loutzenhiser, G (2022) *Tiley on Revenue Law* 10th edn (Hart Publishing).

Mann, FAP (1964) *The Doctrine of Jurisdiction in International Law* (Hague Racueil).

—— (1984) *The Doctrine of International Jurisdiction Revisited after 20 Years* (Hague Racueil).

Markby, W (1996) *Elements of Law* 5th edn (Clarendon Press).

Martha, J (1989) *The Jurisdiction to Tax in International Law: Theory and Practice of Legislative Fiscal Jurisdiction* (Kluwer).

Mill, JS (1861a) 'On the Connection Between Justice and Utility' in *Utilitarianism*.

—— (1861b) *Considerations on Representative Government*.

—— (1871) 'The Principles of Taxation' in Ashley (ed), *Principles of Political Economy with Some of Their Applications to Social Philosophy* 7th edn (AM Kelley).

—— (1909) *Principles of Political Economy with Some of Their Applications to Social Philosophy* (Ashley (ed) AM Kelley).

Murphy, L and Nagel, T (2002) *The Myth of Ownership* (Oxford University Press).

Nozick, R (1974) *Anarchy, State and Utopia* (Basic Books).

Oakeshott, M (1975) *On Human Conduct* (Clarendon).

—— (1999), 'The Rule of Law' in Oakeshott, *On History and Other Essays* (Liberty Fund).

Oliver, Lord (1993) 'Judicial Approaches to Revenue Law' in Gammie and Shipwright (eds), *Striking the Balance: Tax Administration, Enforcement and Compliance in the 1990s* (Institute for Fiscal Studies).

Organisation for Economic Co-operation and Development (2015) *Measuring and Monitoring BEPS: Final Report* (OECD).

—— (2021) *Revenue Statistics Interpretative Guide* (OECD).

—— (2023), *Aggressive Tax Planning* available at <www.oecd.org/tax/aggressive/>.

Penner, JE (1997) *The Idea of Property in Law* (Oxford University Press).

—— (2005) 'Misled by "Property"' 18 *Canadian Journal of Law and Jurisprudence* 75.

Qureshi, AH (1987) 'The Freedom of a State to Legislate in Fiscal Matters Under General International Law' *Bulletin for International Fiscal Documentation* 16.

Qureshi, AH and Kumar, A (2019) *The Public International Law of Taxation: Texts, Cases & Materials* 2nd edn (Wolters Kluwer).

Raphael, DD (2001) *What is Justice* (Oxford University Press).

Rawls, J (1969) 'Two Concepts of Rules in Action' in Acton (ed), *The Philosophy of Punishment* (St. Martin's).

—— (2001) *Justice as Fairness: A Restatement* (Belknap).

Raz, J (1980) *The Concept of a Legal System* 2nd edn (Oxford University Press).

—— (1986) *The Morality of Freedom* (Oxford University Press).

—— (1989) 'Facing Up: A Reply' 62 *Southern California Law Review* 1153.

Reimer, E and Rust, A (eds) (2015) *Klaus Vogel on Double Taxation Conventions* 2nd edn (Wolters Kluwer).

Sales, P (2019) 'Legislative Intention, Interpretation, and the Principle of Legality' 40 *Statute Law Review* 53.

Sedley, S (2015) *Lions Under the Throne* (Cambridge University Press).

Simmel, G (2004) *The Philosophy of Money* 3rd edn, trans Mottonmore and Frisby (Routledge).

Simon's Taxes (Looseleaf: Butterworths LexisNexis).

Smith, A (1776) *The Wealth of Nations*.

Smith, S (2015) *Taxation: A Very Short Introduction* (Oxford University Press).

Snape, J (2011) *The Political Economy of Corporation Tax: Theory, Values and Law Reform* (Hart Publishing).

—— (2017) 'The Legal Interpretation of Tax Law: United Kingdom' in Van Brederode et al (eds), *The Legal Interpretation of Tax Law* (Wolters Kluwer).

—— (2019) '*WT Ramsay* v *Commissioners of Inland Revenue* (1981): Ancient Values, Modern Problems' in Snape and de Cogan (eds), *Landmark Cases in Revenue Law* (Hart Publishing).

Snape, J and Frecknall-Hughes, J (2017) 'John Locke: Property, Tax and the Private Sphere' in Harris and de Cogan (eds), *Studies in the Histories of Tax Law, Volume 8* (Hart Publishing).

Tarrant, J (2011) 'Obligations as Property' 34 *University of New South Wales Law Journal* 11.

Thuronyi, V (ed), (1998) *Tax Law Design and Drafting* (International Monetary Fund).

Thuronyi, V, Brooks, K and Kolozs, B (2016) *Comparative Tax Law* (Kluwer International BV).

Vallentyne, P (2015) 'Taxation, Redistribution and Property Rights' in Marmor (ed), *The Routledge Companion to the Philosophy of Law* (Taylor & Francis).

—— (2018) 'Libertarianism and Taxation' in O'Neill and Orr (eds), *Taxation: Philosophical Perspectives* (Oxford University Press).

Vann, R (1996) 'International Aspects of Income Tax' in Thuronyi (ed), *Tax Law Design and Drafting* (International Monetary Fund).

Wattel, P, Vermeulen, O and Marres, H (2018) *European Tax Law* 7th edn (Wolters Kluwer).

Wintour, P and Syal, R (2012) 'Jimmy Carr tax arrangements "Morally wrong", says David Cameron' *The Guardian* available at <www.theguardian.com/politics/2012/jun/20/jimmy-carr-tax-david-cameron>.

Woodcock, G, Bullock, HL and Kaldor, N (1955) 'Memorandum of Dissent', *Royal Commission on the Taxation of Profits and Income, Final Report*, Cmd 9474 (HMSO).

Worthington, S (2006) 'The Disappearing Divide Between Property and Obligation: The Impact of Aligning Legal Analysis and Commercial Expectation' 42 *Texas International Law Journal* 917.

YouGov (2017) *Tax Avoidance and Tax Evasion* available at: <https://yougov.co.uk/topics/politics/explore/issue/Tax_avoidance_and_tax_evasion?content=surveys>.

TABLE OF CASES